Praise for
Globalization from Below

"*Globalization from Below* is a concise and very readable book that assists the reader in understanding the 'new world order' and its impact on society."

—Edward Asner, actor

"Neophyte or social movement veteran, you need this succinct guide to avoid the pitfalls, ambushes, and ordinary stupidity ready to waylay the well-meaning activist. Thanks to Brecher, Costello, and Smith, we can put winning strategies in their place. We may even get it right this time—and, believe me, this time, it's urgent. Bravo."

—Susan George, author of *A Fate Worse Than Debt*

"This lean, thoughtful, and incisive book examines the most important political question raised by the advent of globalization: will the growth of a broad grassroots protest movement grow, succeed in entering the political lists, and transform the corporate-led global agenda. A must-read for political activists."

—Frances Fox Piven, coauthor of *Poor People's Movements*

"While the media portrays anti-corporate protesters as everything from protectionists to wacko Luddites, the authors of *Globalization from Below* clearly show that our movement is a profoundly humane response to a global economic system gone awry. Their Global Program articulates what we are for—democratic decision making, fair distribution of wealth, environmental sustainability—and how we can continue to weld and strengthen the disparate pieces of this emerging international grassroots movement. *Globalization from Below* gives us direction for turning the tide of the global economy from one that lifts all yachts to one that truly lifts all boats."

—Medea Benjamin, Co-Founder of Global Exchange

Globalization from Below

The Power of Solidarity

Jeremy Brecher

Tim Costello

Brendan Smith

A book from Commonwork:
A Resource and Strategy Project for Globalization from Below

South End Press
Cambridge, Massachusetts

Library of Congress Cataloging-in-Publication Data

Brecher, Jeremy.
Globalization from below : the power of solidarity / Jeremy Brecher, Tim Costello, Brendan Smith.
   p. cm.
   Includes bibliographical references and index.
   ISBN 0-89608-623-2 (hardcover) — ISBN 0-89608-622-4 (pbk.)
   1. Social movements. 2. Globalization. I. Costello, Tim. II. Smith, Brendan, 1972– III. Title.

HN59.2 .B74 2000
303.48'4—dc21

00-061242

South End Press, 7 Brookline Street, #1, Cambridge, MA 02139-4146
www.southendpress.org

05 04 03 02 01   2 3 4 5 6

 PRINTED IN CANADA

Table of Contents

Acknowledgments

We have been extremely fortunate in the comments we have received from those who read an earlier draft of this book. We would like to thank: Andy Banks, Medea Benjamin, Elaine Bernard, John Brown Childs, Tony Clarke, Kevin Danaher, Jonathan Fine, Barbara Garson, Becky Glass, Mike Pertschuk, Mike Prokoch, Jai Sen, Peter Waterman, Susan Wefald, and Frieder Otto Wolf.

Special thanks go to two friends who truly proved the adage that one's critics are one's best friends: Patrick Bond, who argued through many points while this book was being written, and Jai Sen, who provided extensive and valuable critical commentary on the manuscript.

We would like to thank the following for information, encouragement, and other forms of aid: Sarah Anderson, Dennis Brutus, John Cavanagh, Doug Hellinger, Steve Hellinger, Mark Ritchie, and Anna Sofaer.

We would like to thank Jill Cutler for her extensive editorial work.

We would like to thank our editor, Anthony Arnove, and the staff of South End Press for their care in preparing this book and for their long-term commitment to making such work available.

Our greatest debt is to the hundreds of activists in dozens of movements who have been our teachers over the years. Whatever is of merit in this book is mostly attributable to them.

Introduction

Corporations, markets, investors, and elites are going global. The globalization that is so often celebrated by economists, pundits, corporate executives, and the leaders of the world's richest nations is actually their "globalization from above."

Globalization from above can and should be contested by a "globalization from below" through which people at the grassroots around the world link up to impose their own needs and interests on the process of globalization. A movement embodying globalization from below is already emerging. Its global grassroots solidarity has the power to transform the world.

Globalization gets mixed reviews. Greater interconnectedness among the world's people seems to promise a "global village" in which the destructive antagonisms of the past can be left behind, replaced by global cooperation and enriching diversity. The advocates of a world without national economic barriers maintain that it will make everyone, including the people and countries at the bottom, better off.

But the actual experience of fin-de-millennium globalization has not fulfilled this promise. Instead, it has given us more poor people than the world has ever known and increased threats to the environmental conditions on which human life itself depends. It has led many to fear the loss of hard-won social and environmental protections and even of meaningful self-government.

Globalization from above is provoking a worldwide movement of resistance. While this movement has been gathering for years, many people first became aware of it in late 1999, when tens of thousands of protesters brought the Seattle meeting of the World Trade Organization (WTO) to a halt. As the *New York Times* reported,

> The surprisingly large protests in Seattle by critics of the World Trade Organization point to the emergence of a new and vocal coalition ... [that included] not just steelworkers and auto workers, but anti-sweatshop protesters from colleges across the nation and members of church groups, consumer groups, the Sierra Club, Friends of the Earth and the Humane Society.[1]

This movement is neither a one-shot nor a local phenomenon. As Elaine Bernard, executive director of the Harvard Trade Union Program, put it in the *Washington Post,*

> The WTO meeting was merely the place where these people burst onto the American public's radar. Social movements around the world had already linked into grass-roots networks, made possible by the astonishing speed at which they can communicate in the Internet era.[2]

Is such a movement futile, or can it actually affect the course of globalization? The argument of this book is that people can indeed exercise power over globalization, but only by means of a solidarity that crosses the boundaries of nations, identities, and narrow interests. A corporate-driven, top-down globalization can only be effectively countered by globalization from below.

Fortunately, much of the movement that is emerging in response to globalization is showing just such a character. As Naomi Klein wrote in a *New York Times* op-ed,

> The protesters in Seattle have been bitten by the globalization bug as surely as the trade lawyers inside the Seattle hotels ... and they know it. This is the most internationally minded, globally linked movement the world has ever seen.[3]

Nonetheless, this movement is ambivalent about globalization. All of its participants share a commitment to resist globalization in its present form, but they differ on what should replace it. Some aim to roll back globalization and restore the national economies—real or imagined—of the past. Some present an agenda of modest reforms to correct globalization's worst excesses. Some are prepared to embrace a more interconnected, less nationally bounded world—but only one radically different from the "actually existing globalization" being created from above.

We are among those who believe that this movement can only succeed if it evolves from resistance, reform, and restoration to transformation—albeit a transformation that is rooted in today's resistance, that reforms institutions at every level, and that restores those elements of democracy, diversity, and ecological balance that globalization from above has destroyed. Such a transformation requires a multilevel strategy and program to impose new rules on the global economy while transferring wealth and power to ordinary people—a worldwide economic and political democratization.

Why This Book

The emergence of a worldwide social movement for globalization from below changes the conditions of human action. It opens new possibilities for addressing not only globalization from above but also longstanding problems of poverty, oppression, war, and environmental destruction. But it is one thing to initiate a movement; it is something else to change the world. What those new possibilities are and how to utilize them is now the subject of a lively international discussion. This book is intended as a contribution to that dialogue. It lays out a perspective that we believe is already shared by many in this movement and that is implicit in much of what the movement actually does. Our primary purpose is to make that perspective explicit and to spell out its implications so that they can be subject to criticism and improvement.

Conventionally, basic values are the province of priests; policy the province of officials; and strategy the province of the top brass. But in a social movement, people must act on their own initiative and on the basis of their own convictions. So values, policy, and strategy cannot be handed down on a transmission belt from on high, but must be something that people make day by day in the process of determining their own actions.

No movement is born knowing what it thinks, what it wants, and how to achieve its goals. That takes a process, both of experimental action and of thought and discussion.

Any movement develops a self-understanding, whether a tacit set of assumptions expressed primarily in action, a formalized theory, or something in between. This book is intended as a contribution to the self-understanding of the movement that has developed in response to globalization. It presents a perspective on the character, values, goals, and strategy of this emerging movement. We try to place it in the context of a broad understanding of social movements, how they develop, and how they achieve their objectives, drawing on the history of past movements and our own experience as activists in the current movement and a few dozen previous ones. We try to map the terrain on which this movement operates and indicate how it can avoid the many pitfalls and move toward its goals. Whatever the weaknesses of our approach, we hope that this book identifies a set of questions that the movement needs to discuss.

This book was written in the wake of the Battle of Seattle and reflects the significant changes that took place in the politics of globalization at the end of the old millennium. While its concerns are global, its focus no doubt reflects the experience and limitations of the authors not only as Americans, but as residents of southern New England, which has had its own specific experience of globalization.

While we try to articulate a perspective for the movement as a whole, and even more broadly, for all those people who need to change the course of globalization, we would emphasize that there is no privileged position from which to view this whole. Every movement participant—individual or group—will have to put the pieces of the puzzle together for themselves. Indeed, a fundamental tenet of the movement should be that everyone is entitled to participate in the social dialogue on the big questions about the world and its future.

This book reflects, and is limited by, the view from our own vantage point. But however limited their own vantage points, people can learn from each other, can adapt to and incorporate each others' views. We have tried to do so, but our effort is inevitably inadequate. Our fondest hope is that others will criticize it and correct it to accommodate their own views—but do so in a way that also incorporates the needs and perspectives of others.

This book does not aim to present either an introduction to or a complete analysis of globalization. (Our more general analysis of globalization in presented in *Global Village or Global Pillage.*)[4] Nor is it meant as a universal guide for social change. It is focused on the transnational, multi-issue movements emerging at the turn of the millennium in response to globalization from above. Those movements are now only in their early stages of development; we will be delighted if they grow and change so rapidly that they come to transcend much of what is said in this book. In the meantime, we hope this book will be useful to everyone who is fighting against globalization from above.

The Chapters

"Globalization and Its Specter" presents a brief overview of globalization from above and the problems it causes for people and the environment. Then it describes the itineraries through which various constituencies have come to challenge globalization from above and to converge toward a common movement for globalization from below.

"The Power of Social Movements (and Its Secret)" investigates the character of social movements to discover how a movement like globalization from below can possibly affect something so powerful as globalization from above. It examines how social movements arise; how they link initially disparate groups; how they transform power relations; and the pitfalls they face.

"Two, Three, Many Levels" looks at the relation between globalization from below and governmental power. It examines what kind of global governance structure is emerging; discusses the problems with either a global government or a return to conventional national sovereignty; and proposes a multilevel alternative.

"Handling Contradictions in the Movement" considers how the movement for globalization from below can address its contradictions. It examines two controversial issues as examples: the tension between protecting the environment and meeting human needs, and the conflicting needs of people in rich and poor countries.

"A World to Win—for What?" looks at globalization from below's emerging common vision; discusses why that vision needs to be concretized into a common program that can be implemented; and describes how such a program is being constructed.

"Draft of a Global Program" presents one possible version of globalization from below's emerging common program.

"Self-Organization from Below" examines the rise of transnational social movement networks and affinity group–based action organizations, and evaluates their strengths and weaknesses. It looks at the relation of these forms to the movement as a whole and discusses ways the movement can be strengthened organizationally.

"No Movement Is an Island" explores how globalization from below should relate to its allies, the public, the anti-globalization right, electoral politics, governments, regionalism, and those who would make modest reforms in the current system.

"Fix It or Nix It" looks at the interaction between movement initiative and elite response, indicating how the power of the people can be parlayed into social change.

Our "Conclusion" sums up the historical significance of the movement for globalization from below.

•

Globalization is both irreversible and, in its present form, unsustainable. What will come after it is far from determined. It could be a war of all against all, world domination by a single superpower, a tyrannical alliance of global elites, global ecological catastrophe, or some combination thereof. Human agency—what people choose to do—can play a role in deciding between these futures and more hopeful ones.

Acronyms Used

AIDS	Acquired Immune Deficiency Syndrome
AFL-CIO	American Federation of Labor–Congress of Industrial Organizations
CEO	Chief Executive Officer
CONGOs	Coopted nongovernmental organizations
DAN	Direct Action Network
FTAA	Free Trade Area of the Americas
EU	European Union
G-7	Group of Seven Nations
G-77	Group of Seventy-Seven Nations
G-8	Group of Eight Nations
GDP	Gross Domestic Product
GEO	Genetically engineered organism
GNP	Gross National Product
HIPC	Heavily Indebted Poor Countries
ILO	International Labor Organization
IMF	International Monetary Fund
LDCs	Less developed countries
NAFTA	North American Free Trade Agreement
MAI	Multilateral Agreement on Investment
NLC	National Labor Committee
NGO	nongovernmental organization
OECD	Organization for Economic Cooperation and Development
PNTR	Permanent Normal Trade Relations
PP21	People's Plan for the Twenty-First Century
UN	United Nations
UNCTAD	United Nations Conference on Trade and Development
UNDP	United Nations Development Program
UNEP	United Nations Environment Program
WDCs	Wrongly developed countries
WTO	World Trade Organization

Chapter 1

Globalization and Its Specter

Globalization from Above

Epochal changes can be difficult to grasp—especially when you are in their midst. Those who lived through the rise of capitalism or the industrial revolution knew something momentous was happening, but just what was new and what it meant were subjects of confusion and debate.

In a sense, there has been a global economy for 500 years. But the last quarter of the 20th century saw global economic integration take new forms. At first, globalization manifested itself as apparently separate and rather marginal phenomena: the emergence of the "Eurodollar market," "off-shore export platforms," and "supply-side economics," for example. It was easy to separate out one or another aspect of globalization—such as the growth of trade or of international economic institutions—and see it as an isolated phenomenon. These seemingly peripheral developments, however, gradually interacted in ways that changed virtually every aspect of life and defined globalization as a new global configuration.[1]

Globalization was not the result of a plot or even a plan. It was caused by people acting with intent—seeking new economic opportunities, creating new institutions, trying to outflank political and economic opponents. But it resulted not just from their intent, but also from unintended side effects of their actions and the consequences of unintended interactions.[2] Future historians will note at least the following aspects of the globalization process:

Production: In the 1970s, corporations began building factories and buying manufactured products in low-wage countries in the third world on a vastly expanded scale. Such off-shore production grew into today's "global assembly line," in which the components of a shirt or car may be made and assembled in a dozen or more different countries. Direct investment abroad by "American" companies has grown so rapidly that the value of the goods and services they produce and sell outside the United States is now three times the total value of all American exports.[3]

Markets: Corporations came increasingly to view the entire world as a single market in which they buy and sell goods, services, and labor. In 1973, barely 12 percent of world output entered international trade. By 1996, this had virtually doubled to 23.6 percent.[4]

Finance: Starting with the rise of the Eurodollar market in the 1970s, international capital markets have globalized at an accelerating rate. More than $1.5 trillion flows daily across international borders.[5] Private financial flows to developing countries grew from $44 billion in 1990 to $256 billion in 1997.[6]

Technology: New information, communication, and transportation technologies—computers, satellite communications, containerized shipping, and, increasingly, the Internet—have reduced distance as a barrier to economic integration. Furthermore, the process of creating new technologies has itself become globalized.[7]

Global institutions: The World Trade Organization (WTO), the International Monetary Fund (IMF), the World Bank, and similar institutions at a regional level have developed far greater powers and have used them to accelerate the globalization process.

Corporate restructuring: While corporations have always operated internationally, starting in the 1980s they began to restructure in order to operate in a global economy. New corporate forms—strategic alliances, global outsourcing, captive suppliers, supplier chains, and, increasingly, transnational mergers—allowed for what the economist Bennett Harrison has called the "concentration of control [with] the decentralization of production."[8]

Changing structure of work: Globalization has been characterized by a "re-commodification of labor" in which workers have increasingly lost all rights except the right to sell their labor power. All over the world, employers have downsized, outsourced, and made permanent jobs into contingent ones. Employers have attacked job security requirements, work rules, worker representation, healthcare, pensions, and other social benefits, and anything else that defined workers as human beings and employers as partners in a social relationship, rather than simply as buyers and sellers of labor power.

Neoliberal ideology and policies: Starting with monetarism and supply-side economics, globalization has been accompanied—and accelerated—by an emerging ideology now generally known as neoliberalism or the Washington consensus. It argues that markets are efficient and that government intervention in them is almost always bad. The policy implications—privatization, deregulation, open markets, balanced budgets, deflationary austerity, and dismantling of the welfare state—were accepted by or imposed on governments all over the world.

Changing role of the state: While some governments actively encouraged globalization and most acquiesced, globalization considerably reduced the power of nation states, particularly their power to serve the interests of their own people. Capital mobility undermined the power of national governments to pursue full employment policies or regulate corporations. International organizations and agreements increasingly restricted environmental and social protections. Neoliberal ideology reshaped beliefs about what government should do and what it is able to accomplish.

Neo-imperialism: Globalization reversed the post–World War II movement of third world countries out of colonialism toward economic independence. Globalization has restored much of the global dominance of the former imperialist powers, such as Western Europe, Japan, and, above all, the United States. With the collapse of Communism, that dominance has also spread to much of the formerly Communist world. Globalization has taken from poor countries control of their own economic policies and concentrated their assets in the hands of first world investors. While it has enriched some third world elites, it has subordinated them to foreign corporations, international institutions, and dominant states. It has intensified economic rivalry among the rich powers.[9]

Movement of people: While people have always crossed national borders, the economic disruptions and reduction of national barriers caused by globalization are accelerating migration. International travel and tourism have become huge industries in their own right.

Cultural homogenization: Globalization has undermined the economic base of diverse local and indigenous communities all over the world. Growing domination of global media by a few countries and companies has led not to greater diversity, but to an increasingly uniform culture of corporate globalism.

As *New York Times* columnist and globalization advocate Thomas Friedman summed up, we are in a new international system: "Globalization is not just a trend, not just a phenomenon, not just an economic fad. It is the international system that has replaced the cold-war system." The driving force behind globalization is free-market capitalism: "Globalization means the spread of free-market capitalism to virtually every country in the world."[10]

The Contradictions of Globalization from Above

The proponents of globalization promised that it would benefit all: that it would "raise all the boats." Workers and communities around the globe were told that if they downsized, deregulated, eliminated social services, and generally became more competitive, the benefits of globalization would bless them. The poorest and most desperate were promised that they would see their standard of living increase if they accepted neoliberal austerity measures. They kept their end of the bargain, but globalization from above did not reciprocate. Instead, it is aggravating old and creating new problems for people and the environment.

Even conventional economic theory recognizes that the "hidden hand" of the market doesn't always work. Unregulated markets regularly produce unintended side effects or "externalities"—such as ecological pollution for which the producer doesn't have to pay, or the devastation of communities when corporations move away.

Unregulated markets also produce unintended interaction effects, such as the downward spirals of depressions and trade wars. Unregulated markets do nothing to correct inequalities of wealth; indeed, they often intensify the concentration of wealth, leading to expanding gaps between rich and poor.[11] Globalization from above has globalized these problems, while dismantling at every level the non-market institutions that once addressed them.

Globalization promotes a destructive competition in which workers, communities, and entire countries are forced to cut labor, social, and environmental costs to attract mobile capital. When many countries each do so, the result is a disastrous "race to the bottom."

The race to the bottom occurs not just between developing and developed worlds, but increasingly among the countries of the third world. Consider the case of Argentina and Brazil. Early in 1999, Brazil devalued its currency by 40 percent. A *New York Times* reporter in Argentina found that "[a]bout 60 manufacturing companies have moved to Brazil in recent months, seeking lower labor costs and offers of tax breaks and other government subsidies." Companies closing Argentine factories to supply the Argentine market from Brazil included Tupperware, Goodyear, and Royal Philips Electronics. The Argentine auto and auto-parts industries suffered a 33 percent loss of production and a 59 percent fall in exports in 1999. "General Motors, Ford Motor and Fiat are all transferring production to Brazil."[12]

Argentine President Fernando De la Rua commented, "If you ask me what is my chief concern in a word, that word is 'competitiveness.'" The measures he has taken to become more "competitive" exemplify the race to the bottom. "The crown jewel of the De la Rua economic policy is his labor reform" intended to "reduce the bargaining power of labor unions and help businesses more easily hire and fire new workers."

But this gutting of labor rights was not enough to protect Argentine manufacturers against products from lower-wage countries. A shoe manufacturer who expected the new labor law to cut his labor costs by 10 percent "felt constrained because of the competitive disadvantage he continued to suffer in relation to Brazilian shoe producers who pay their workers one-third the wage an Argentine shoemaker earns." The director of a medical supply company who was considering closing his plant observed that it was impossible to compete with the flood of cheap Korean and Chinese syringes in recent years and that Brazilian officials were offering a package of tax breaks and subsidized loans to relocate to Brazil.

The role of international institutions in promoting the race to the bottom is illustrated by the fact that both Brazil and Argentina were shaping their economic policies in accord with loan agreements they had made with the IMF.

First world countries are also engaged in the race to the bottom. Over the past two decades, for example, the United States made huge cuts in corporate taxes while slashing federal funding for health, education, and community development. Canada, which did not make equivalent cuts, found that its tax structure was "making it difficult for companies to compete internationally. Many businesses have simply moved across the border to the US." In response, Canada decided in early 2000 to lower its corporate tax rate from 28 percent to 21 percent. In a fit of ingratitude, the Business Council on National Issues, representing Canada's 150 largest companies, condemned the cuts as "timid." The Business Council's president opined that "[t]he strategy should be to provide an environment more attractive than the US now." The disappointed chief executive of an e-commerce services company said he had been planning to open offices in Calgary, Alberta, and Vancouver, British Columbia, but that after the inadequate tax cuts he was leaning toward Chicago or Minneapolis instead. The director of the Canadian Taxpayers Federation observed, "There's competition for tax cuts, just like everything else."[13]

The race to the bottom brings with it the dubious blessings of impoverishment, growing inequality, economic volatility, the degradation of democracy, and destruction of the environment.

Impoverishment: The past quarter-century of globalization has seen not a reduction but a vast increase in poverty. According to the 1999 UN *Human Development Report,* more than 80 countries have per capita incomes lower than they were a decade or more ago.[14] James

Wolfensohn, president of the World Bank, says that, rather than improving, "global poverty is getting worse. Some 1.2 billion people now live in extreme poverty."[15] Global unemployment is approaching 1 billion.[16]

In the United States, the downward pressures of globalization are manifested in the stagnation of wages despite the longest period of economic growth in American history. Real average wages were $9 per hour in 1973; 25 years later, they were $8 per hour. The typical married-couple family worked 247 more hours per year in 1996 than in 1989—more than six weeks' worth of additional work each year.[17]

Inequality: Globalization has contributed to an enormous increase in the concentration of wealth and the growth of poverty both within countries and worldwide. Four hundred and forty-seven billionaires have wealth greater than the income of the poorest half of humanity. In the United States, the richest man has wealth equal to that of the poorest 40 percent of the American people.[18] The net worth of the world's 200 richest people increased from $440 billion to more than $1 trillion in just the four years from 1994 to 1998. The assets of the three richest people were more than the combined GNP of the 48 least developed countries.[19]

The downward pressures of globalization have been focused most intensively on discriminated-against groups that have the least power to resist, including women, racial and ethnic minorities, and indigenous peoples. Women have been the prime victims of exploitation in export industries and have suffered the brunt of cutbacks in public services and support for basic needs. Immigrants and racial and ethnic minorities in many parts of the world have not only been subject to exploitation, but have been abused as scapegoats for the economic troubles caused by globalization from above. Indigenous people have had their traditional ways of life disrupted and their economic resources plundered by global corporations and governments doing their bidding.

Volatility: Global financial deregulation has reduced barriers to the international flow of capital. More than $1.5 trillion now flows across international borders daily in the foreign currency market alone. These huge flows easily swamp national economies. The result is a world economy marked by dangerous and disruptive financial volatility.

In 1998, for example, an apparently local crisis in Thailand rapidly spread around the globe. In two years, Malaysia's economy shrunk by 25 percent, South Korea's by 45 percent, and Thailand's by 50 percent. Indonesia's economy shrunk by 80 percent; its per capita gross domestic product dropped from $3,500 to less than $750; and 100 million people—nearly half of the population—sank below the poverty line.[20] According to former World Bank chief economist Joseph Stiglitz,

> Capital market liberalization has not only not brought people the prosperity they were promised, but it has also brought these crises, with wages falling 20 or 30 percent, and unemployment going up by a factor or two, three, four or ten.[21]

Degradation of democracy: Globalization has reduced the power of individuals and peoples to shape their destinies through participation in democratic processes.

Of the 100 largest economies in the world, 51 today are corporations, not countries.[22] Globalization has greatly increased the power of global corporations relative to local, state, and national governments. The ability of governments to pursue development, full employment, or other national economic goals has been undermined by the growing ability of capital to simply pick up and leave.

There are few international equivalents to the anti-trust, consumer protection, and other laws that provide a degree of corporate accountability at the national level. As a result, corporations are able to dictate policy to governments, backed by the threat that they will relocate.

Governmental authority has been undermined by trade agreements such as NAFTA and the WTO and by international financial institutions such as the IMF and World Bank, which restrict the power of national, state, and local governments to govern their own economies. These institutions are all too often themselves complicit in the denial of human rights. (At a time when 100 to 200 Algerians were having their throats cut every week, the IMF stated, "Directors agree that Algeria's exemplary adjustment and reform efforts deserve continued support of the international financial community.")[23] They make decisions affecting billions of people, but they are largely free of democratic control and accountability. As one unnamed WTO official was quoted by the *Financial Times*, "The WTO is the place where governments collude in private against their domestic pressure groups."[24]

Environmental destruction: Globalization is accelerating ecological catastrophe both globally and locally. Countries are forced to compete for investment by lowering environmental protections in an ecological race to the bottom. (Seventy countries have rewritten their mining codes in recent years to encourage investment.[25]) Neoliberal policies imposed by international institutions or voluntarily accepted by national governments restrict environmental regulation. Worldwide, corporations promote untested technologies, such as pesticides and genetic engineering, turning the planet into a testing lab and its people into guinea pigs. Growing poverty leads to desperate overharvesting of natural resources.

Global corporations' oil refineries, chemical plants, steel mills, and other factories are the main source of greenhouse gases, ozone-depleting chemicals, and toxic pollutants. Overfishing of the world's waters, overcutting of forests, and abuse of agricultural land result from the search for higher corporate profits, the drive to increase exports, and the increase in poverty.

Globally, environmental destruction is changing the basic balances on which life depends. Carbon dioxide has reached record levels in the atmosphere.[26] Global warming is already resulting in the melting of glaciers, the dying of coral reefs, climate instability, and "a disturbing change in disease patterns."[27] An estimated one-quarter of the world's mammal species and 13 percent of plant species are threatened with extinction in the worst period of mass extinction of species in 65 million years.[28]

•

It is often said that globalization is inevitable and that there is no alternative. But, in fact, the new global regime is highly vulnerable. It violates the interests of the great majority of the world's people. It lacks political legitimacy. It is riven with divisions and conflicting interests. It has the normal crisis-prone character of capitalist systems, but few of the compensatory non-market institutions that helped stabilize pre-globalization economies. And it has few means to control its own tendency to destroy the natural environment on which it—and its species—depend. These are the reasons that, as the *Financial Times* wrote, the world had swung "from the triumph of global capitalism to its crisis in less than a decade."[29]

Globalization from Below

Just as the corporate and political elites are reaching across national borders to further their agendas, people at the grassroots are connecting their struggles around the world to impose their needs and interests on the global economy. Globalization from above is generating a worldwide movement of resistance: globalization from below.[30]

Throughout the 20th century, nationally based social movements have placed limits on the downsides of capitalism. Workers and communities won national economic regulation and protections ranging from environmental laws to labor unions and from public investment to progressive taxation.

Globalization outflanked both national movements and national economies. It caused a historic break in the institutions, traditions, and movements that had opposed unfettered capitalism since its inception. Not only Communism, but also social democracy, economic nationalism, trade unionism, and democratic government itself were rolled back by the neoliberal tide—and often found their own foundations crumbling from within in the face of forces they could not understand or control.

Nonetheless, the real problems of a system of unrestrained capitalism did not disappear. Globalization only intensified them. And so the impulses that had generated these counter-movements in the first place began to stir.

Like globalization from above, these counter-movements began from many diverse starting points, ranging from local campaigns against runaway plants to union organizing in poor countries, and from protection of indigenous peoples to resistance to corporate-

engineered food. Their participants have come to the issues of globalization by way of many different itineraries. For example:
• Acid rain and global warming do not respect national borders. They have forced environmentalists around the world to recognize global ecological interdependence.[31] At the same time,
environmentalists became increasingly conscious that the actions of
global corporations and of institutions such as the World Bank destroyed local environments—symbolized by the destruction of the
Amazon rain forest and India's Narmada Valley. While some argued
that globalizing capitalism would actually promote environmental-
ism in the third world, environmentalists discovered that it was instead creating an environmental race to the bottom as countries
lowered environmental standards to attract corporations. The
WTO's anti-environmental rules—symbolized by its decision con-
demning a US law for the protection of sea turtles—brought the environmental movement into direct confrontation with this central
institution of globalization.
• In the 1970s, the world's poorer countries formed the
G-77 and initiated a North-South Dialogue with the rich countries to
formulate a New International Economic Order. When the rich
countries withdrew from this effort in the 1980s and began instead
to promote neoliberal policies coordinated through the IMF, World
Bank, and WTO, most third world governments went along with
their plans, albeit in many cases reluctantly. But networks of third
world NGOs continued to develop an alternative agenda and to press
it both on their own countries and on international institutions.
Third world governments have recently begun to follow their lead.
As the rich countries prepared their agenda for the 1999 Seattle WTO
extravaganza, poor-country governments began to question
whether they had benefitted from globalization. Encouraged by the
global citizens' movement to halt any new round of WTO negotiations, third world delegations for the first time refused to go along
with the rich countries' proposals until their own concerns were addressed, helping to bring the meeting down in shambles. Early in
2000, the G-77 held its first ever head-of-state–level meeting and proposed an alternative program that included debt relief, increased aid,

access to technology, and a shift in economic decision making from the World Bank and IMF to the UN.[32]

• People in rich countries have a long history of compassionate assistance for poor countries—sometimes in alliance with religious proselytizing and colonialism. With the development of the third world debt crisis in the 1980s, however, many people of conscience in the first world became deeply concerned about the effect of crushing debts on third world people and began to demand cancellation of their debt. Many then went on to address the broader question of the devastating "structural adjustment" policies being imposed on the debtor countries by the IMF, World Bank, and rich countries.

• When negotiations started in 1986 for what became the WTO, critics argued that US and other first world proposals would benefit agribusiness and transnational commodity traders, but would drive millions of small farmers in both the North and South off their farms. Advocates for small farmers around the world began holding regular counter-meetings at the negotiations and developed a global network to oppose the proposals. They provided much of the core for international opposition to the emerging WTO. What has been described as "the first really global demonstration," in December 1990, brought farmers from Europe, Japan, North America, Korea, Africa, and Latin America to Brussels—helping force the negotiations into deadlock.[33] Since then, small farmers have been at the forefront of opposition to WTO agricultural policies, efforts to turn seeds into private property, and genetically engineered organisms (GEOs).

• From World War II until the 1960s, the labor movement in the United States was a strong supporter of economic liberalization, both as an expression of its alliance with US international policy and as a means to secure expanding markets for US-made products. Faced with a massive loss of jobs in auto, steel, garment, and other industries in the 1970s, the labor movement increasingly campaigned for tariffs and other barriers to imports designed to "save American jobs." Over the 1990s, globalization made such economic nationalist strategies less and less credible. Organized labor increasingly moved toward demanding reform of the global economy as a whole, symbolized by demands for labor rights and environmental standards in international trade agreements to protect all the world's workers and communities from the race to the bottom. Its participation in the Seattle WTO protests represented a new page in US labor history and was followed by the announcement of a long-term "Campaign for Global Fairness."

• The burgeoning identity-based movements of the late 20th century found that many identities did not respect national borders. The women's movement slogan "sisterhood is powerful" evolved into a consciousness that "sisterhood is global." A growing awareness of the global oppression of women led to a struggle to define women's rights as internationally protected human rights. Events surrounding the UN's 1995 Beijing women's conference brought large numbers of women in the United States to an awareness of the impact of IMF and World Bank–imposed structural adjustment austerity programs on women in poor countries, and their similarity to the implications of welfare reform for poor women in the United States. The fact that the great majority of those exploited in overseas factories were young women led to a growing concern about the global sweatshop.

• From the 1960s on, consumer movements in many countries had enshrined a wide range of protections in national laws and had developed effective legal techniques for imposing a degree of accountability on corporations. Consumer organizations—notably Ralph Nader's Public Citizen—discovered that trade agreements like NAFTA and the WTO were overriding high national standards for such things as food and product safety. They also realized that both neoliberal ideology and competition among countries for investment were tending to lower consumer protection standards all over the world. New consumer issues, such as the right of governments to regulate genetically engineered food, have steadily increased consumer concern over globalization.

• African American communities in the US have been concerned with conditions in Africa from the mid-19th century to the struggle against South African apartheid. But the 1990s saw two specific concerns that brought attention to the global economy. The first was the devastation wreaked on African countries by international debt and the brutal structural adjustment conditionalities the IMF and World Bank imposed on African countries in exchange for helping them roll over their debts. The other was the struggle over the African trade bill (known to its critics as the "NAFTA for Africa" bill) that ostensibly opened US markets to African exports but in fact imposed more stringent structural adjustment–type conditions while doing little to provide desperately needed debt relief. Many African American leaders, including a wide swath of black clergy, became involved in the Jubilee 2000 debt relief campaign and the fight against the "NAFTA for Africa" bill and for an alternative proposed by Rep. Jesse Jackson, Jr.

• Groups in Europe, Japan, and the US that had been involved in support for development and popular movements in third world countries found those countries increasingly used as production platforms by global corporations. They began calling attention to the growth of sweatshops and pressuring companies like the Gap and Nike to establish acceptable labor and human rights conditions in their factories around the world. Their efforts gradually grew into an anti-sweatshop movement with strong labor and religious support and tens of thousands of active participants. In the US, college students took up the anti-sweatshop cause on hundreds of campuses, ultimately holding sit-ins on many campuses to force their colleges to ban the use of college logos on products not produced under acceptable labor conditions.

Many other people are following their own itineraries toward globalization from below. Some, such as activists in the human rights movement seeking to protect rights of people globally, or public health advocates trying to control tobacco companies and provide AIDS treatment for poor countries, are just as globalized as those described above. Some, such as activists in the immigrant networks spreading out around the world, are in some ways even more global and are challenging globalization from above by their very way of life. Some, like the tens of millions who have participated in nationally organized mass and general strikes and upheavals, are resisting the effects of globalization from above, even if (so far) they are doing so in a national framework.[34] Far more numerous still are the billions of people who are being adversely affected by globalization from above, but who have not yet found their own way to respond. Ultimately, their itineraries may be the most important of all.

Confluence

From diverse origins and through varied itineraries, these movements now find themselves starting to converge. Many of their participants are recognizing their commonalties and beginning to envision themselves as constructing a common movement.

This convergence is occurring because globalization is creating common interests that transcend both national and interest-group boundaries. As author and activist Vandana Shiva wrote in the wake of the Battle of Seattle,

> When labour joins hands with environmentalists, when farmers from the North and farmers from the South make a common commitment to say "no" to genetically engineered crops, they are not acting as special interests. They are defending the common interests and common rights of all people, everywhere. The divide and rule policy, which has attempted to pit consumers against farmers, the North against the South, labour against environmentalist has failed.[35]

Much of the convergence is negative: different groups find themselves facing the same global corporations, international institutions, and market-driven race to the bottom. But there is also a growing positive convergence around common values of democracy, environmental protection, community, economic justice, equality, and human solidarity.

Participants in this convergence have varied goals, but its unifying goal is to bring about sufficient democratic control over states, markets, and corporations to permit people and the planet to survive and begin to shape a viable future. This is a necessary condition for participants' diverse other goals.

Is this confluence a movement, or is it just a collection of separate movements? Perhaps it can most aptly be described as a movement in the early stages of construction. Within each of its components there are some people who see themselves as part of a global, multi-issue movement and others who do not. Those who do are often networked with their counterparts in other movements and other countries. Their numbers are increasing rapidly and they are playing a growing role within their movements and organizations. They are developing a shared vision. And they see themselves as constructing a common movement. It is this emerging movement that we refer to as globalization from below.

Globalization from below is certainly a movement with contradictions. Its participants have many conflicting interests. It includes many groups that previously defined themselves in part via negative reference to each other. It includes both rigidly institutionalized and wildly unstructured elements.

Globalization from below is developing in ways that help it cope with this diversity. It has embraced diversity as one of its central values, and asserts that cooperation need not presuppose uniformity. Its structure tends to be a network of networks, facilitating cooperation without demanding organizational centralization.

Older orientations toward charitable "us helping them" on the one hand, and narrow self-interest on the other, are still present; but there is also a new recognition of common interests in the face of globalization. Solidarity based on mutuality and common interest increasingly forms the basis for the relationships among different parts of the movement.

The movement is generally multi-issue, and even when participants focus on particular issues, they reflect a broader perspective. As Howard Zinn wrote of the Seattle WTO protests,

> In one crucial way it was a turning point in the history of movements of the recent decades—a departure from the single-issue focus of the Seabrook occupation of 1977, the nuclear-freeze gathering in Central Park in 1982, the great Washington events of the Million-Man March, [and] the Stand for Children [march].[36]

Globalization from below has now established itself as a global opposition, representing the interests of people and the environment worldwide. It has demonstrated that, even when governments around the world are dominated by corporate interests, the world's people can act to pursue their common interests.

Globalization from below grew both out of previous movements and out of their breakdown. There is much to be learned from the historical heritage of centuries of struggle to restrain or replace capitalism, and today's activists often draw on past values and practices in shaping their own. But it would be a mistake to simply treat this new movement as an extension of those that went before—or to attach it to their remnants.[37]

Globalization in all its facets presents new problems that the old movements failed to address. That is part of why they declined so radically. It also presents new opportunities that will be lost if the new wine is simply poured back into the old bottles. Besides, the historic break provides an invaluable opportunity to escape the dead hand of the past and to reground the movement to restrain global capital in the actual needs and conditions of people today.[38]

Globalization from below is now a permanent feature of the globalization epoch. Even if its current expressions were to fail, the movement would rise again, because it is rooted in a deep social reality: the need to control the forces of global capital.

Chapter 2

The Power of Social Movements (and Its Secret)

The supporters of globalization from above control most of the world's governments. They control the global corporations and most of the world's wealth. They have a grip on the minds of people all over the world. It seems inconceivable that they can be effectively challenged.

Yet social movements have overcome equal or even greater concentrations of wealth and power in the past. Colonized peoples from North America to India, and Africa to Vietnam, have thrown out imperial powers with many times their wealth and firepower. The abolitionist movement eliminated slavery in most of the world and the civil rights movement eliminated legal segregation in the United States. In recent decades, mass movements have brought down powerful dictatorships from Poland to the Philippines. A coordinated domestic and global movement abolished South African apartheid. To understand how social movements are able to overcome what seem to be overwhelming forces, we need to take a deeper look at the processes underlying such successes.

How Social Movements Arise

Normally, most people follow life strategies based on adapting to the power relations of their world, not on trying to change them. They do so for a varying mix of reasons, including:

- Belief that existing relations are good and right.

• Belief that changing them is impossible.

• Fear that changing them would lead to something worse.

• An ability to meet their own needs and aspirations within existing power relations.

• Belief that existing power relations can and will change for the better.

• Identification with the dominant groups or with a larger whole—for example, a religion or nation.

• Fear of sanctions for violation of social rules or the will of the powerful.[1]

Most institutions and societies have elaborate systems for assuring sufficient consent or acquiescence to allow their key institutions to function. These means of maintaining a preponderance of power—often referred to as "hegemony"—range from education to media, and from elections to violent repression.[2]

Over time, problems with existing social relationships may accumulate, initiating a process of change. These problems usually affect particular social groups—for example, particular communities, nations, classes, racial, ethnic and gender groups, religious and political groupings, and the like. The process may start with some people internally questioning or rejecting some aspects of the status quo. It becomes a social process as people discover that others are having similar experiences, identifying the same problems, asking the same questions, and being tempted to make the same rejections. Then people begin to identify with those others and to interact with them. This turns what might have been an individual and isolating process into a social one.[3]

Seeing that other people share similar experiences, perceptions, and feelings opens a new set of possibilities. Perhaps collectively we can act in ways that have impacts isolated individuals could never dream of having alone. And if we feel this way, perhaps others do, too.

This group formation process constructs new solidarities. Once a consciousness of the need for solidarity develops, it becomes impossible to say whether participants' motives are altruistic or selfish, because the interest of the individual and the collective interest are no longer in conflict; they are perceived as one.[4]

This process occurs not only in individuals, but also in groups, organizations, and constituencies.

Thus form social movements.[5]

Why Social Movements Can Be Powerful

The fact that people develop common aspirations doesn't mean that they can realize them. Why are social movements able to change society? The power of existing social relations is based on the active cooperation of some people and the consent and/or acquiescence of others. It is the activity of people—going to work, paying taxes, buying products, obeying government officials, staying off private property—that continually re-creates the power of the powerful.

Bertolt Brecht dramatized this truth in his poem "German War Primer":

> General, your tank is a strong vehicle.
> It breaks down a forest and crushes a hundred people.
> But it has one fault: it needs a driver.[6]

This dependence gives people a potential power over society—but one that can be realized only if they are prepared to reverse their acquiescence.[7] The old American labor song "Solidarity Forever" captures the tie between the rejection of acquiescence and the development of collective power:

> They have taken untold millions
> that they never toiled to earn
> But without our brain and muscle
> not a single wheel can turn.
> We can break their haughty power,
> gain our freedom when we learn
> That the union makes us strong.[8]

Social movements can be understood as the collective withdrawal of consent to established institutions.[9] The movement against globalization from above can be understood as the withdrawal of consent from such globalization.

Ideally, democracy provides institutionalized means for all to participate equally in shaping social outcomes. But in the rather common situation in which most people have little effective power over established institutions, even those that claim to be democratic, people can still exercise power through the withdrawal of consent. Indeed, it is a central means through which democratization can be imposed.

Withdrawal of consent can take many forms, such as strikes, boycotts, and civil disobedience. Gene Sharp's *The Methods of Nonviolent Action* lists no fewer than 198 such methods, and no doubt a few have been invented since it was written.[10] Specific social relations create particular forms of consent and its withdrawal. For example, WTO trade rules prohibit city and state selective purchasing laws like the Massachusetts ban on purchases from companies that invest in Burma—making such laws a form of withdrawal of consent from the WTO, in effect an act of governmental civil disobedience.[11] (Several foreign governments threatened to bring charges against the Massachusetts Burma law in the WTO before it was declared unconstitutional by the US Supreme Court in June 2000.)

The World Bank depends on raising funds in the bond market, so critics of the World Bank have organized a campaign against purchase of World Bank bonds, modeled on the successful campaign against investment in apartheid South Africa. Concerted refusal of impoverished debtor countries to continue paying on their debts—for example, through a so-called debtors' cartel—would constitute a powerful form of withdrawal of consent from today's global debt bondage.

Just the threat of withdrawal of consent can be an exercise of power. Ruling groups can be forced to make concessions if the alternative is the undermining of their ultimate power sources.[12] The movement for globalization from below has demonstrated that power repeatedly. For example, the World Bank ended funding for India's Narmada Dam when 900 organizations in 37 countries pledged a campaign to defund the Bank unless it canceled its support. And Monsanto found that global concern about genetically engineered organisms so threatened its interests that it agreed to accept the Cartagena Protocol to the Convention on Biological Diversity, allowing GEOs to be regulated.[13]

At any given time, there is a balance of power among social actors.[14] Except in extreme situations like slavery or military occupation, unequal power is reflected not in an unlimited power of one actor over the other. Rather, it is embedded in the set of rules and practices that are mutually accepted, even though they benefit one far more than the other. When the balance of power is changed, subordinate groups can force change in these rules and practices.

The power of the people is a secret that is repeatedly forgotten, to be rediscovered every time a new social movement arises. The ultimate source of power is not the command of those at the top, but the acquiescence of those at the bottom. This reality is hidden behind the machinations of politicians, business leaders, and politics as usual. The latent power of the people is forgotten both because those in power have every reason to suppress its knowledge and because it seems to conflict with everyday experience in normal times. But when the people rediscover it, power structures tremble.

Linking the Nooks and Crannies

New movements often first appear in small, scattered pockets among those who are unprotected, discriminated against, or less subject to the mechanisms of hegemony. They reflect the specific experiences and traditions of the social groups among which they arise. In periods of rapid social change, such movements are likely to develop in many such milieus and to appear very different from each other as a result. In the case of globalization from below, for example, we have seen significant mobilizations by French chefs concerned about preservation of local food traditions, Indian farmers concerned about corporate control of seeds, and American university students concerned about school clothing made in foreign sweatshops. Even if in theory people ultimately have power through withdrawal of consent, how can such disparate groups ever form a force that can exercise that power?

One common model for social change is the formation of a political party that aims to take over the state, whether by reform or by revolution. This model has always been problematic, since it implied the perpetuation of centralized social control, albeit control exercised in the interest of a different group.[15] However, it faces further difficulties in the era of globalization.

Reform and revolution depend on solving problems by means of state power, however acquired. But globalization has outflanked governments at local and national levels, leaving them largely at the mercy of global markets, corporations, and institutions. Dozens of parties in every part of the world have come to power with pledges to overcome the negative effects of globalization, only to submit in a matter of months to the doctrines of neoliberalism and the "discipline of the market." Nor is there a global state to be taken over.[16]

Fortunately, taking state power is far from the only or even the most important means of large-scale social change. An alternative pathway is examined by historical sociologist Michael Mann in *The Sources of Social Power*.[17] The characteristic way that new solutions to social problems emerge, Mann maintains, is neither through revolution nor reform. Rather, new solutions develop in what he calls "interstitial locations"—nooks and crannies in and around the dominant institutions. Those who were initially marginal then link together in ways that allow them to outflank those institutions and force a reorganization of the status quo.

At certain points, people see existing power institutions as blocking goals that could be attained by cooperation that transcends existing institutions. So people develop new networks that outrun them. Such movements create subversive "invisible connections" across state boundaries and the established channels between them.[18] These interstitial networks translate human goals into organizational means.

If such networks link groups with disparate traditions and experiences, they require the construction of what are variously referred to as shared worldviews, paradigms, visions, frames, or ideologies. Such belief systems unite seemingly disparate human beings by claiming that they have meaningful common properties:

> An ideology will emerge as a powerful, autonomous movement when it can put together in a single explanation and organization a number of aspects of existence that have hitherto been marginal, interstitial to the dominant institutions of power.[19]

The emerging belief system becomes a guide for efforts to transform the world. It defines common values and norms, providing the basis for a common program.[20] When a network draws together people and practices from many formerly marginal social spaces and makes it possible for them to act together, it establishes an independent source of power. Ultimately, new power networks may become strong enough to reorganize the dominant institutional configuration.

The rise of labor and socialist movements in the 19th century and of feminist and environmental movements in the 20th century in many ways fits this model of emergence at the margins, linking, and outflanking.[21] So, ironically, does the emergence of globalization from above as described in the previous chapter.

Self-organization in marginal locations and changing the rules of dominant institutions are intimately linked. The rising European bourgeoisie both created their own market institutions and fought to restructure the political system in ways that would allow markets to develop more freely. Labor movements both organized unions and forced governments to protect labor rights, which in turn made it easier to organize unions.

Over time, movements are likely to receive at least partial support from two other sources. Some institutions, often ones that represent similar constituencies and that themselves originated in earlier social movements but have become rigidified, develop a role of at least ambiguous support. And sectors of the dominant elites support reforms and encourage social movements for a variety of reasons, including the need to gain support for system-reforming initiatives and a desire to win popular backing in intra-elite conflicts.

Social movements may lack the obvious paraphernalia of power: armies, wealth, palaces, temples, and bureaucracies. But by linking from the nooks and crannies, developing a common vision and program, and withdrawing their consent from existing institutions, they can impose norms on states, classes, armies, and other power actors.

The Lilliput Strategy

How do these broad principles of social movement–based change apply to globalization from below? In fact, they describe the very means by which it is being constructed. We call this the Lilliput Strategy, after the tiny Lilliputians in Jonathan Swift's fable *Gulliver's Travels* who captured Gulliver, many times their size, by tying him up with hundreds of threads.

In response to globalization from above, movements are emerging all over the world in social locations that are marginal to the dominant power centers. These are linking up by means of networks that cut across national borders. They are beginning to develop a sense of solidarity, a common belief system, and a common program. They are utilizing these networks to impose new norms on corporations, governments, and international institutions.

The movement for globalization from below is, in fact, becoming an independent power. It was able, for example, to halt negotiations for the Multilateral Agreement on Investment (MAI), to block the proposed "Millennium Round" of the WTO, and to force the adoption of a treaty on genetically engineered products. Its basic strategy is to say to power holders, "Unless you accede to operating within these norms, you will face threats (from us and from others) that will block your objectives and undermine your power."

The threat to established institutions may be specific and targeted withdrawals of support. For example, student anti-sweatshop protestors have made clear that their campuses will be subject to sit-ins and other forms of disruption until their universities agree to ban the use of school logos on products made in sweatshops. Or, to take a very different example, in the midst of the Battle of Seattle, President Bill Clinton, fearing loss of electoral support from the labor movement, endorsed the use of sanctions to enforce international labor rights.[22] The threat may, alternatively, be a more general social breakdown, often expressed as fear of "social unrest."[23]

The slogan "fix it or nix it," which the movement has often applied to the WTO, IMF, and World Bank, embodies such a threat. It implies that the movement (and the people of the world) will block the globalization process unless power holders conform to appropriate global norms. This process constitutes neither revolution nor conventional "within the system" and "by the rules" reform. Rather, it constitutes a shift in the balance of power.

As the movement grows in power, it can force the modification of institutions or the creation of new ones that embody and/or impose these norms as enforceable rules.[24] For example, the treaties on climate change and on genetic engineering force new practices on corporations, governments, and international institutions that implement norms propounded by the environmental and consumer movements. Student anti-sweatshop activists force their universities to join an organization that bans university logos on products made under conditions that violate specified rules regarding labor conditions. The world criminal court, endorsed by many countries under pressure of the global human rights movement, but resisted by the United States, would enforce norms articulated at the Nuremberg war crimes tribunal.

These new rules in turn create growing space for people to address problems that the previous power configuration made insoluble. Global protection of human rights makes it easier for people to organize locally to address social and environmental problems. Global restrictions on fossil fuels that cause global warming, such as a carbon tax, would make it easier for people to develop renewable energy sources locally.

While the media have focused on global extravaganzas like the Battle of Seattle, these are only the tip of the globalization from below iceberg. The Lilliput Strategy primarily involves the building of solidarity among people at the grassroots. For example:

• Under heavy pressure from the World Bank, the Bolivian government sold off the public water system of its third largest city, Cochabamba, to a subsidiary of the San Francisco–based Bechtel Corporation, which promptly doubled the price of water for people's homes. Early in 2000, the people of Cochabamba rebelled, shutting down the city with general strikes and blockades. The government declared a state of siege and a young protester was shot and killed. Word spread all over the world from the remote Bolivian highlands via the Internet. Hundreds of e-mail messages poured into Bechtel from all over the world demanding that it leave Cochabamba. In the midst of local and global protests, the Bolivian government, which had said that Bechtel must not leave, suddenly reversed itself and signed an accord accepting every demand of the protestors. Meanwhile, a local protest leader was smuggled out of hiding to Washington, DC, where he addressed the April 16 rally against the IMF and World Bank.[25]

• When the Japanese-owned Bridgestone/Firestone (B/F) demanded 12-hour shifts and a 30 percent wage cut for new workers in its American factories, workers struck. B/F fired them all and replaced them with 2,300 strikebreakers. American workers appealed to Bridgestone/Firestone workers around the world for help. Unions around the world organized "Days of Outrage" protests against B/F. In Argentina, a two-hour "general assembly" of all workers at the gates of the B/F plant halted production while 2,000 workers heard American B/F workers describe the company's conduct. In Brazil, Bridgestone workers staged one-hour work stoppages, then "worked like turtles"—the Brazilian phrase for a slowdown. Unions in Belgium, France, Italy, and Spain met with local Bridgestone managements to demand a settlement. US B/F workers went to Japan and met with Japanese unions, many of whom called for the immediate reinstatement of US workers. Five hundred Japanese unionists marched through the streets of Tokyo, supporting B/F workers from the US. In the wake of the worldwide campaign, Bridgestone/Firestone unexpectedly agreed to rehire its locked out American workers.[26]

• In April 2000, AIDS activists, unions, and religious groups were poised to begin a lawsuit and picketing campaign denouncing the Pfizer Corporation as an AIDS profiteer for the high price it charges for AIDS drugs in Africa. Pfizer suddenly announced that it would supply the drug fluconazole, used to control AIDS side effects, for free to any South African with AIDS who could not afford it. A few weeks later, US, British, Swiss, and German drug companies announced that they would cut prices on the principal AIDS drugs, anti-retrovirals, by 85 to 90 percent. Meanwhile, when South Africa tried to pass a law allowing it to ignore drug patents in health emergencies, the Clinton administration lobbied hard against it and put South Africa on a watch list that is the first step toward trade sanctions. But then, according to the *New York Times,* the Philadelphia branch of Act Up, the gay advocacy group, decided

> to take up South Africa's cause and start heckling Vice President Al Gore, who was in the midst of his primary campaign for the presidency. The banners saying that Mr. Gore was letting Africans die to please American pharmaceutical companies left his campaign chagrined. After media and campaign staff looked into the matter, the administration did an about face

and accepted African governments' circumvention of AIDS drug patents.[27]

• Two independent unions, the United Electrical Workers Union (UE) in the United States and the Frente Autentico del Trabajo (FAT) in Mexico, formed an ongoing Strategic Organizing Alliance in the mid-1990s. At General Electric (GE) in Juarez, FAT obtained the first secret ballot election in Mexican labor history, aided by pressure on GE in the United States. The trinational Echlin Workers Alliance was formed to jointly organize Echlin, a large multinational auto parts corporation, in Canada, Mexico, and the US. In cooperation with Mexican unions, US unions brought charges under the NAFTA side agreements for the repression of Echlin workers. A rank-and-file activist from FAT traveled to Milwaukee, Wisconsin, to help UE organize foundry workers of Mexican origin. Workers from each country have repeatedly conducted speaking tours organized by those across the border. US workers helped fund and build a Workers' Center in Juarez. And the Cross-Border Mural Project has developed binational teams that have painted murals celebrating international labor solidarity on both sides of the border.[28]

How Movements Go Wrong

It is nowhere guaranteed that any particular social movement will succeed in using its potential power to realize the hopes and aspirations of its participants or to solve the problems that moved them to action in the first place. There are plenty of pitfalls along the way.

Schism: From Catholic and Protestant Christians to Sunni and Shiite Muslims, from Communists and socialists to separatists and integrationists, social movements are notorious for their tendency to split. They can often turn into warring factions whose antagonisms are focused primarily on each other. Splits often occur over concrete issues but then perpetuate themselves even when the original issues are no longer salient.

Repression: Movements can be eliminated, or at least driven underground, by legal and extralegal repression.

Fading out: The concerns that originally drew people into a movement may recede due to changed conditions. An economic upswing or the opening of new lands has often quieted farmer movements. Or constant frustration may simply lead to discouragement and withdrawal.

Leadership domination: In a mild form, the movement evolves into an institution in which initiative and control pass to a bureaucratized leadership and staff, while the members dutifully pay their dues and act only when told to do so by their leaders. In a more virulent form, leaders establish a tyrannical control over members.[29]

Isolation: Movements may become so focused on their own internal life that they are increasingly irrelevant to the experience and concerns of those who are not already members. Such a movement may last a long time as a sect but be largely irrelevant to anyone except its own members.

Cooptation: A movement may gain substantial benefits for its constituency, its members, or its leaders, but do so in such a way that it ceases to be an independent force and instead comes under the control of sections of the elite.

Leadership sell-out: Less subtly, leaders can simply be bought with money, perks, flattery, opportunities for career advancement, or other enticements.

Sectarian disruption: Movements often fall prey to sects that attempt either to capture or to destroy them. Such sects may emerge from within the movement itself or may invade it from without.

•

To succeed, globalization from below must avoid these pitfalls; promote movement formation in diverse social locations; establish effective linkages; develop a sense of solidarity, a common worldview, and a shared program; and utilize the power that lies hidden in the withdrawal of consent.

Chapter 3

Two, Three, Many Levels

Globalization from above has altered the framework within which social action occurs. As we saw in Chapter 1, it is vastly increasing the power of global corporations and markets, limiting the authority of governments, and empowering international institutions that have virtually no democratic accountability. These changes pose questions about political authority that are new in human history and that require those who would challenge globalization from above to think in new ways.

Discussion of what to do about globalization is haunted by an apparent dichotomy between strengthening global institutions and reinforcing national sovereignty. At one pole are those who argue that globalization is moving toward a world state, and that this tendency should be supported:

> A world polity of global institutions, for the first time ever in world history, is becoming capable of directing the processes of the modern world-system.... While the idea of a world state may be a frightening specter to some, we are optimistic about it.[1]

At the other pole are those who argue that "the interests of workers and eco-social movements across the world are now, unequivocally, to stop and reverse the process of the construction of a global state that serves only capital's interests."[2] They call instead for a withdrawal from the global economy and a reassertion of national economic sovereignty.

This dichotomy, fortunately, is false. The real choice is not between global and national authority but between a globalization from above that disempowers people at every level and a globalization from below that expands self-government not only at a global level but at regional, national, and local levels, as well.

Globalization and the State

Globalization is creating not a world state but a complex, multilevel polity in which the familiar categories of national sovereignty vs. world government are rendered less and less relevant by a system of "overlapping authority and multiple loyalty."[3] That system's elements include not only nations and a wide range of global institutions, but supranational regional institutions such as NAFTA and the EU and local, subnational, and cross-border entities that have growing autonomy in many parts of the world. They also include less formalized structures, notably the power nexus centered in the US Treasury Department, which functions almost as one flesh and blood with US-based corporations and investors and exercises preponderant influence over the World Bank, IMF, WTO, and G-7.

This emerging polity resembles less a world state than the multilevel, overlapping polity of medieval Europe before the rise of the nation state.[4] Nation states, especially the most powerful nation states, remain powerful actors, but they hardly exercise the "final and absolute authority" that classically defines sovereignty.[5]

While global institutions such as the WTO, IMF, and World Bank have acquired many powers once reserved for national governments, globalization is much more than such global institutions. An adequate strategy must address not only international institutions but the race to the bottom, the power of global corporations, the destructive volatility of global capital, and the dominant rule of the rich governments and the interests they serve.

The Limits of National Economic Sovereignty

The idea of restoring national economic sovereignty comes in many political complexions. A leftwing version envisions withdrawal from the global economy and its institutions as a way to allow progressive domestic policies and national economic development.[6] A rightwing version sees it as a way to reestablish national assertiveness and domestic social order.[7] A third world version calls for the "delinking" of national economies from the global economy.[8]

Globalization from above has unquestionably undermined some of the most valuable functions of both national governments and national economies. Reconstructing them will play a crucial part in correcting the damage done by globalization. The idea of restoring national economic sovereignty, however, does not provide an adequate framework for addressing the problems of globalization.

Nowhere to hide

For those who see institutions such as the WTO, IMF, and World Bank as the central feature of globalization and the main expression of what's wrong with it, the obvious solution is to "get these institutions off our backs" by abolishing them or by having their countries withdraw from them.

Unfortunately, these institutions represent only a small part of the process of globalization and a small part of the problem that globalization makes for people and the environment. Global markets were developing and corporations were going global years before the development of NAFTA and the WTO. International financial capital was putting desperate squeezes on debtor countries well before the IMF stepped in to manage and rationalize the process.

While these institutions certainly attempt to manage the global economy in the interest of capital, and certainly accelerate the globalization process, withdrawing from them or abolishing them is unlikely to alter the basic dynamics of global capitalism. In particular, it will not alter four dynamics that are most devastating for working people, the global poor, and the environment:

• global competition to lower labor, environmental, and social costs (the global race to the bottom);

• the power of highly mobile capital to pour into a country, create an economic bubble, and then devastate it by withdrawing;

• the bargaining power of corporations vis-à-vis governments; or

• the power concentrated in the nexus that links the US Treasury, corporations, and global institutions such as the WTO, IMF, and World Bank.

Without some strategy to address these problems, people and nations will continue to be at the mercy of global capital, even if the WTO, IMF, and World Bank disappear tomorrow.

Globalization trumps national regulation

The advocates of national economic sovereignty often see it as a way to escape international pressures that impose neoliberal economic policies. They hope to make less austere, more growth-oriented national policies possible. The historical experience of the era of globalization, however, is that capital mobility sharply limits the ability of even the richest and most powerful countries to pursue expansionary full-employment policies.

When one country stimulates its economy, the result has tended not to be expanded domestic jobs and growth, but rising imports and inflation. Jimmy Carter and François Mitterand both tried stimulative growth strategies but encountered inflation, trade deficits, and financial crises, and abandoned the attempt. It even happened to Margaret Thatcher. As Steven Rattner put it, "When the British economy was stimulated [in 1986], the result was not higher domestic output but higher imports and higher inflation."[9] Investor pressure similarly forced President Bill Clinton to abandon the expansionary program on which he was elected in the early 1990s.[10]

Since that time, global economic integration, especially global financial mobility, has become so great that the effects of stimulative national policies are hard even to identify. The huge Japanese expansionary public spending initiative of the late 1990s had little long-term effect, except perhaps in buoying the stock market in the United States. And the US economy boomed despite a federal budget surplus.

Dangers of nationalist economic strategies

An inappropriate emphasis on national sovereignty plays into the hands of rightwing nationalists such as Pat Buchanan and Jean-Marie

Le Pen who oppose anything that interferes with the sovereign right of their nation to do anything it wants, regardless of the effect on others. This conflicts with the need to limit national power by such means as global environmental regulation, the treaty banning land mines, the global criminal court, and national obligations under the UN Charter to eschew armed aggression.[11]

Unilaterally imposed protective tariffs and related forms of protectionism are a logical means for delinking and a probable outcome of the abolition of a multilateral trading system. Even Patrick Bond, a proponent of delinking, acknowledges, "It wouldn't be hard to envisage latter-day Smoot-Hawley–style protective tariffs kicking off a downward spiral of trade degeneration reminiscent of the early 1930s."[12]

There is also a danger in turning over the global arena to an unimpeded globalization from above. The movement's ability to mobilize in the global arena to block elite schemes and to pursue its own objectives is significant, as evidenced in the blocking of the MAI and the signing of the international agreement on GEOs. To shift attention from the global to the national arena is to abandon the capacity to affect the global arena and turn it over to unfettered globalization from above.

The current predicament is largely a result of the fact that globalization allowed capital to "outflank" labor, popular movements, and nation states. A central need is to develop means of counter-flanking capital. And that can hardly be a retreat to a framework of national reform. As the geographer David Harvey put it,

> Withdrawing to the nation-state as the exclusive strategic site of class organization and struggle is to court failure (as well as to flirt with nationalism and all that that entails). This does not mean the nation-state has become irrelevant—indeed it has become more relevant than ever. But the choice of spatial scale is not "either or" but "both/and" even though the latter entails confronting serious contradictions.[13]

A particularly catastrophic example of this danger was the response to the global economic crisis of 1998–1999. Massive struggles against IMF-imposed policies marked by incredible heroism and suffering took place on a national basis in countries such as South Korea and Indonesia. But these were largely isolated from each other and presented no united front to the IMF and the Western creditors it represented. The debtor countries and their social movements generally functioned within a national arena. The idea of a debtors' cartel was hardly even considered, although just discussing such a possibility would have considerably increased the leverage of debtor countries. Instead, the IMF was able to say to each country, "Play ball with us or your markets will be stolen by other countries." An alternative transnational strategy for dealing with the crisis could have reframed the entire struggle in a way that was foreclosed by the emphasis on the national level and on individual nations' relations to international institutions.

Consensus and Divergence in the Movement

How can the movement for globalization from below escape the simplistic national vs. global or local vs. global dichotomies?

Broad areas of consensus exist within the movement that opposes globalization from above. There is almost universal opposition to the coercive functions exercised by the World Bank, the IMF, and the WTO in the interests of global capital. Few believe that these institutions should be able to order governments to cut public health programs or ban boycotts of repressive regimes. Further, most of the movement—in sharp distinction to neo-nationalists such as Pat Buchanan—strongly supports the principles underlying the UN, notwithstanding the obvious need for reform in the organization.[14] In fact, most in both first and third world countries support a stronger role for the UN in global economic regulation.

Further, virtually the entire movement supports policies, such as national development programs and currency controls, that strengthen the ability of national governments to counteract the power of global economic forces. There is broad support for the empowerment of local people to have control over their own lives and resources, and for the organization of workers and oppressed groups in civil society, even when that is opposed by their national governments. Finally, there is near-universal support for social movement organization that crosses national borders and unites people around the globe.

There are, however, sharp differences within the movement on how much emphasis to put on strengthening local communities, national governments, and global institutions. Some emphasize the need for a global system that provides minimum rights and standards and new forms of global economic regulation.[15] Others emphasize the need to restore the power of the nation state to control national economies. Still others portray localization—the economic empowerment of local communities—as the true alternative to globalization.[16] And some emphasize the significance of units that are not generally represented by governments, such as subnational and supranational regions or tribal, ethnic, religious, and linguistic groups that may cut across national borders.

Parallel to this tension is divergence over the appropriate roles of the state and civil society. For some, the restoration of the power of governments over corporations and markets is a central objective. For others, the empowerment of workers, communities, and other civil society actors—vis-à-vis their own governments, as well as global economic actors and forces—is equally or more important.

Beyond these substantive questions there are what might be called differences of stance. Some take a stance of resistance to globalization: let's fight the forces of globalization until they are annihilated or at least until they give up and go away. Some take a stance of restoration: let's go back to a world in which our community or our country didn't have to worry about these global forces and actors. Some (we among them) take a more welcoming attitude toward growing global interconnection in principle, but seek to give it a very different form.

These differences are not purely cognitive; they often have a strong emotional component tied to senses of personal and group identity. Different people put different values on the strength to say no, the desire to protect threatened relationships and ideals, and the openness to new experiences and connections.

These differences also imply different alliances. Some in the US labor movement, for example, pursue an alliance with the Democratic Party represented by Clinton and Al Gore, despite its admitted dominance by global corporate interests, on the grounds that such an alliance can be the vehicle for incorporating labor and environmental protections in international trade rules. Some in the consumer movement have made common cause with the nationalist right, represented by people like Patrick Buchanan, arguing that it expresses a rejection of globalization, global economic institutions, and excessive corporate power.[17]

A Multilevel Alternative

The apparent opposition among strengthening local, national, and global institutions is based on a false premise: that more power at one level of governance is necessarily disempowering to people at others. But today the exact opposite is the case. The empowerment of local and national communities and polities today *requires* a degree of global regulation and governance. Far from being dichotomous, they are interdependent. Globalization from below requires a framework that recognizes that interdependence.

Global capital has usurped powers that rightfully belong to people and to their representatives in government. The challenge is for people to establish greater control over their economic lives by establishing greater control over global capital. To do so requires a stronger governmental role *and* increased organization in civil society at every level from local to global. These various levels of action, far from being in competition, can actually be mutually supportive. Indeed, the programs needed at each level are unlikely to work for long unless complemented by supportive polices and structures at the other levels.

Consider, for example, the issue of local empowerment. In the United States, ironically, local empowerment has been a major theme of that part of the right that is most favorable to global capitalism. Newt Gingrich, as conservative Republican speaker of the US House of Representatives, campaigned to eliminate federal regulations that "interfered" with states and municipalities. Of course, the real purpose of this faux localism was to break down regulations that establish minimum wages and labor standards, preserve the envi-

ronment, reduce poverty, and protect the rights of women, oppressed minorities, the disabled, and trade unions. "Empowering
local communities" meant putting them at the mercy of powerful
corporations and financiers. It also meant pitting them against each
other in a race to the bottom. Clearly, national regulation that protects minimum standards and limits the race to the bottom actually
strengthens, rather than undermines, the ability of people in local
communities to control their own lives.

The same can be true globally. While the rules and policies currently imposed by the IMF, World Bank, and WTO empower corporations and disempower people at every level, that doesn't mean that
different global institutions and policies couldn't have the opposite
effect. For example, international agreements that reduce gases that
destroy the ozone layer and produce global warming can protect local communities and countries against environmental destruction.
Global economic institutions that regulate global demand and international currency flows would strengthen the ability of national governments to regulate their own economies. Environmental and
labor conditions in international trade agreements could put limits
on the race to the bottom. So could trade union agreements with
corporations specifying minimum conditions worldwide. Enforceable international codes of conduct for corporations could reduce
their ability to dictate conditions to countries and communities.[18]

In fact, such higher-level regulation is essential if the forces of
globalization are to be tamed. This point is missed by those who see
globalization simply as a matter of greater power for international
economic institutions. Globalization was not caused (even though it
was accelerated) by the WTO or NAFTA. And globalization will continue even if such institutions are abolished.

Indeed, the likely result of completely eliminating supranational
economic regulation is not genuine national self-determination but an
economic war of all-against-all. As each nation pursues policies of
economic nationalism, others will follow suit in escalating trade
wars. And without means for regulating demand, global depression
is more than likely to follow.

A centralized global state is not required to address these problems. Indeed, the difficulty of establishing such an institution and the equally important difficulty of making it democratically accountable make such a state a dubious objective for the advocates of globalization from below. But supranational regulation does not require such centralization; the pattern of overlapping authority and multiple loyalties that is now emerging suggests the possibility of a system of checks and balances within an emerging global polity.[19] As Filipino activist and scholar Walden Bello put it,

> Today's need is not another centralized global institution, reformed or unreformed, but the deconcentration and decentralization of institutional power and the creation of a pluralistic system of institutions and organizations interacting with one another amid broadly defined and flexible agreements and understandings.[20]

Instead of counterposing local, national, global, and other levels of power , advocates of globalization from below should argue for a strengthening in both state and civil society at every level of those non-market functions that are necessary to protect people and planet. People need to be empowered at every level vis-à-vis corporations and the market. The needed non-market functions should be initiated at any appropriate level, in state and/or civil society, in ways that strengthen the grassroots movement and raise those at the bottom.[21]

Subsidiarity

Such a multilevel, functional approach has been summed up in the "subsidiarity principle." While this principle has been formulated in a variety of ways, it states in essence that decisions should be made "as close to the locus of the actual activity being decided as possible."[22] The European Parliament's Environment Committee describes subsidiarity as "the principle by which democratic involvement is maximized in policymaking, implementation, and enforcement, and by which decisions are taken at the most local level."[23] As political scientist Joseph Henri Jupille explains,

Subsidiarity fundamentally delinks politics from territory.... According to the subsidiarity principle, authority, power, autonomy are elements that may reside in as restricted a space as one individual and in as wide a space as the entire globe. Political authorities overlap and inhabit the same space, and the relationship between them is nonhierarchical—it is one of "interconnectedness rather than nestedness."[24]

Under the subsidiarity principle, "either devolution or centralization may take place, depending upon the particular issue under discussion." In the EU, for example,

While subsidiarity may call for an [EU] approach to transfrontier waste shipments or to environmental issues of global importance, it might on the other hand rule out [EU] action on such issues as the quality of (local) bathing water.[25]

The agencies in charge of local bathing water or global environmental issues need not be governments, though they are part of a governance system; they need specific powers, but not the full trappings of a state.

In sum, the movement for globalization from below should project a positive vision of a different kind of global order, a multilevel form that empowers people at the grassroots level. A guiding principle should be to pursue synergism among the levels—to pursue changes in ways that support each other at different levels. This involves strengthening certain aspects of both government and civil society at every level, while restricting others. It involves not only public policy at various levels but also transnational movements in civil society that aim to transform existing structures so that they begin to grapple with the real problems of redistributing wealth and power and protecting people and the planet.[26]

States and People in the Era of Globalization

The discussion on levels of governance is only part of a wide-ranging dialogue on the fundamentals of political authority that is being generated by globalization from below. This dialogue is redefining the basic concepts of sovereignty and the rights and duties of states, international institutions, and citizens.

Sovereignty is being redefined not as the absolute right of states, but rather as a right of peoples at multiple levels. For example, a post-Seattle statement signed by hundreds of organizations around the world ("WTO—Shrink or Sink!") called for "the sovereignty of peoples and national and subnational democratic decision-making processes."[27] Such a usage redefines sovereignty as a relative rather than an absolute authority.

The human right of an individual or group to influence decisions that affect them is less and less seen as limited to the right of citizens to affect their own government.[28] This broadened concept of the human right to particpate in decision making has been described as a "transborder participatory democracy" that declares "a universal right which recognizes no borders": "the right of the people to intervene in, to modify, to regulate, and ultimately to control any decisions that affect them."[29]

The tension between the historically established sovereign rights of states and the needs of people and environment in the era of globalization requires a modified conception of political legitimacy, one based on the duty of governments at every level to protect human rights and the environment. This shift is partially reflected in UN Secretary-General Kofi Annan's statement that "[g]lobalization and international co-operation are changing our understanding of state sovereignty: states are now widely understood to be the servants of their peoples, and not vice versa."[30]

Under the UN Charter on the Economic Rights and Duties of States, governments have the obligation to protect the human rights of their citizens.[31] These include their labor, social, environmental, economic, and cultural rights. Governments have the right to pursue policies necessary to fulfill these rights.

In a global economy, international coordination and institutions are at times necessary to make it possible for local and national governments to effectively meet their obligations to their own people and exercise the rights necessary to do so. Thus, the redefinition of the rights of states as rooted in their responsibilities leads back to and reinforces the concept of a multilevel world order.

Illegitimate Authorities

The legitimacy of states and therefore their sovereign rights is dependent on, and limited by, their actual representation of their peoples and their conformity with such obligations as the UN Charter and the protection of human rights and the environment. In reality, however, states are largely and increasingly subject to corruption and coercion by global corporations, so that they represent the latter far more than their own people. At present, few if any states could be proven not to be illegitimate outlaw states.

To the extent that global institutions represent states, therefore, they largely represent the global corporations that have usurped control of them. The legitimacy of international institutions such as the IMF, World Bank, and WTO therefore cannot be justified simply by asserting that their authority is delegated by legitimate states. Retiring IMF head Michel Camdessus told a reporter, "If anyone is the voice of the people, it is me. I am elected by 185 countries. I am the one who can claim legitimacy."[32] But such a theory is less and less acceptable. As one commentary put it, "Aside from displaying his breathtaking arrogance, Camdessus' reaction highlights the fatal flaw of the UN system: it is based on an assumption of the legitimacy of governments." But "the elite knows that there is a crisis of legitimacy in institutions and governments."[33]

The legitimacy of both states and international institutions is now contaminated by corruption, usurpation, and bias. It is therefore the obligation of the people—in this case, the people of the world—to "alter or abolish them." Given such an obligation, there must also be a right to take the action necessary to fulfill it. Further, institutional structures, practices, and purported laws that block or punish such action are inherently illegitimate and unconstitutional. They represent little more than lawless force and violence.

These concepts legitimate a withdrawal of consent of the kind that, as we saw in the preceding chapter, provides the underlying power of social movements.

Chapter 4

Handling Contradictions in the Movement

Globalization from above has created common interests among an extraordinary range of people, but that doesn't mean they don't also have conflicting ones. The movement for globalization from below inherits a multitude of national, ethnic, religious, political, and economic conflicts from the pre-globalization era. Further, the globalization process itself creates new conflicts. Finally, social movements can generate their own internal conflicts.

The movement's opponents can be counted on to try to exacerbate these divisions at every opportunity—witness, for example, the concerted effort of WTO officials to portray the demands of first world trade unions for international labor rights as an attack on the poor of the third world. Globalization from below will only succeed if it can unify diverse groups that are hurt by globalization into a cooperating force.

Fostering that cooperation involves:

Dialogue: The most perfect program is no substitute for the give and take in which people assimilate each other's experiences and concerns and try to integrate them with their own. This process requires that participants keep in mind both their own particular interests and the broader common interests of the movement as a whole. Such a dialogue has been a continuing emphasis of globalization from below, represented, for example, in the teach-ins of the International Forum on Globalization and the NGO meetings that have accompanied meetings of WTO, IMF, G-7, and other international organizations all over the world.

Mutual aid: International solidarity has played a central role in the construction of globalization from below. For example, people around the world put pressure on the World Bank to defund the Narmada Dam, which would have forced tens of thousands of rural Indians from their homes. Pressure from workers in Japan, Europe, and Latin America saved the jobs of locked out Bridgestone/Firestone workers in the United States.[1]

Joint struggles: The identification of common enemies and co-operation in opposing them has led disparate groups to new understandings of their common interests. The joint struggle of environmentalists and trade unionists from both the North and the South to block a new round of WTO trade negotiations, for example, led many to see these groups less as antagonists than as allies against globalization from above.

Common norms: Any particular decision produces gains and losses that are distributed differently among different people. People are more willing to accept losses if they occur within a context that provides overall fairness and mutual benefit. For example, polls show that three-quarters of Americans are willing to pay substantially more for a garment that is certified as not having been made in a sweatshop.[2] A world based on the principles of economic and environmental justice is ultimately in the interest of the great majority of people everywhere.

Common programs: In many instances, the existing social structure puts different interests into conflict in ways that can only be resolved in the context of broader social changes. For that reason, a project and program of transformation is a key means for developing unity among different social forces. Ongoing discussion and negotiation have already gone a long way toward sketching a common program for globalization from below. This process is represented in such documents as the "Alternative for the Americas," PP21, the NGO statement from the 2000 UNCTAD meetings, "WTO—Shrink or Sink! The Turn Around Agenda," and many more.[3] (Many of these proposals are synthesized in Chapter 6.)

Cultural accommodation: Conflicts involve not only ideas, interests, and values but also living people with specific cultural meanings and identities. A positive attitude toward diversity has been crucial to the movement's ability to bring together people from different backgrounds. For example, Jubilee 2000 events have been characterized by ecumenical religious services in which literally dozens of religious traditions participate in the way they choose.

Conflict attenuation: Not all conflicts can be eliminated. Successful movements need to cultivate mutual respect for differences, an openness to compromise, an awareness that each of us is fallible, an agreement to disagree, and a willingness to pursue disagreements in appropriate forums that do not disrupt the cooperation needed in other spheres.

Fostering cooperation is not just a task for leaders meeting at international conferences. It is something that every movement participant can contribute to at every level. It can involve so modest an act as sitting down with someone from another group to talk through a sore point that has led to conflict. And it can involve so local an act as developing a community plan for sustainable development that integrates varied economic, social, and environmental needs into a common program.

In the remainder of this chapter, we examine two conflicts that have been divisive for advocates of globalization from below and then look at the interrelation of the two. Our purpose is to illustrate the kinds of approaches needed to address the myriad divergences within the movement.

Human Need vs. the Environment

From the origins of the modern environmental movement in the 1960s, efforts at environmental protection have repeatedly come into conflict with efforts to expand employment through economic development and economic growth. This happens in specific situations—for example, conflict between West Coast lumbering and protection of old-growth forests, or between jobs of Appalachian miners and restrictions on high-sulfur coal, or between the protection of the Amazon jungle and the need of Brazilians for jobs building roads and farms. It also comes in a more general form: growth may provide jobs, but it also may have come to the point where it is unsustainable, overreaching the limits of the environment.

Despite this evident conflict, there have also been extensive efforts to build bridges between environmentalists and labor and other movements that address human needs. The fruits of this work could be seen in the Battle of Seattle, where "Teamsters and Turtles United at Last" was a slogan made flesh.

Part of the groundwork for that unity was laid by an extraordinary coalition effort by workers and environmentalists in the West. For more than 10 years, environmental activists have been battling the Texas-based multinational Pacific Lumber/Maxxam Corporation, trying to stop the destruction of California's old-growth redwood forests. Two people have died and thousands have gone to jail over an issue that many saw as a choice between saving trees and saving jobs. At the same time, steelworkers employed by the same company—Maxxam's Kaiser Aluminum Corporation—were increasingly being pressured by management to accept wage cuts in the name of global competitiveness. When the union finally drew the line and demanded a cost-of-living increase, Kaiser Aluminum forced a strike and locked out 2,900 members of the Steelworkers union in five cities.[4]

Then a funny thing happened. An activist from the militant environmental group Earth First! visited the strikers and tipped them off about an impending hearing on Pacific Lumber's logging plans. One of the strikers drove to the hearing and testified that "Charles Hurwitz was the common enemy," both destroying the forests and abusing his aluminum workers. He received a standing ovation from an audience that included hundreds of nonunion loggers who had been paid to show up by Pacific Lumber.[5]

Recognizing their common interests and goals in making corporations more accountable for their behavior, locked out Steelworkers from Kaiser Aluminum and environmental leaders in California and Oregon formed the Alliance for Sustainable Jobs and the Environment to build a partnership fighting for the protection of both people and the planet.[6] Workers convinced environmentalists to use union printers; environmentalists convinced the workers to use recycled paper.

In April 1999, 50 labor and environmental leaders came together for the first summit of the Alliance, organizing, among other events, joint training workshops and public rallies in Houston, Texas, in the days before Maxxam's annual shareholder meeting. The Steelworkers have recently joined the Environmental Protection Information Center and the Sierra Club in filing lawsuits against Pacific Lumber/Maxxam, based on the net loss of jobs resulting from unsustainable forestry. Finally, at the Battle of Seattle, the Alliance hosted a joint rally and teach-in of environmentalists and Steelworkers.[7]

Such mutual outreach can be initiated at the most local level by an act so simple as dropping by to tip off a supposed "enemy" about an upcoming opportunity. According to Steelworkers' district director David Foster, "The thing that is most important and moving about it all was that it was driven by rank-and-file steelworkers, who'd lived inside aluminum smelters all their lives. This was entirely their idea."[8]

Part of the resolution to conflict between environmental needs and economic needs lies in a recognition that they are not somehow needs of two different sets of people. We all have to make a living. None of us can live on air, no matter how clean. But we all have to live in the environment; you can't cure an asthmatic kid by giving him or her a job or save coastal areas from global warming–caused flooding by economic growth.

Another part of the resolution needs to be worked out day by day over specific issues. For example, when energy-related corporations mobilized against an international climate change treaty limiting greenhouse gases, they found a willing ally in much of the US labor movement. The United Mine Workers, United Food and Commercial Workers, Teamsters, and other unions formed Unions for Jobs and the Environment, which was started with a grant from a consortium of coal and railroad companies. The AFL-CIO attacked the Kyoto Protocol on global warming. That split the labor-environmental alliance—not to mention putting the future of the biosphere at risk. Was there an alternative? Both labor and environmental groups could instead have presented an alternative program for reducing greenhouse gases while creating new, environmentally sound jobs for those displaced.[9]

An interesting political model here might have been the tobacco control movement, which proposed legislation to provide substantial economic assistance for tobacco farmers hurt by anti-smoking policies. Tobacco control advocates argued that reducing smoking was a social good, but that its cost should not be placed on the shoulders of the tobacco farmers. Many environmentalists now support the concept of a "Just Transition" in which the costs of environmental protection are carried by society, not by the people who happen to work in an affected industry.[10]

The term "sustainable development," popularized in 1990 by the World Commission on Environment and Development (the Brundtland Commission), embodies the interdependence of economic and environmental concerns.[11] Since then, a worldwide discussion has made that interdependence clear. The tension between human needs and environmental protection requires new forms of economic regulation and development that reorient economic activity toward halting and repairing environmental damage. The challenge is to develop an alternative economic strategy based on directing work to meeting social needs in environmentally sustainable ways.

Such an approach does not require that the labor movement abandon its traditional goal of full employment for all who want it. But it does require alternatives to full employment based on conventional economic growth. The movement for globalization from below should pursue full employment based on an alternative development path: the environmental reconstruction of society. Such a path would actually reduce the kinds of production that are environmentally and socially destructive. Full employment would surely be both possible and necessary were working hours reduced, adequate services made available, and work redirected to meeting social needs in environmentally sustainable ways.[12] Simply meeting the requirements of the climate change treaty limiting greenhouse gas emissions would lead to a net addition of nearly 800,000 jobs in the United States.[13]

North vs. South

The division between wealthy first world countries largely concentrated in the North and impoverished third world countries concentrated in the South is a historical legacy of centuries of imperialism. Globalization has complicated this picture, increasing poverty in much of the North, the former Soviet Union, and more than 100 third world countries while raising living standards in a dozen or so third world countries. The overall gap between rich and poor countries has grown rapidly in the era of globalization, presenting a serious challenge to a movement based on common interests of people in the North and South.

Globalization itself has been presented as a solution to the problems of poverty and development, but its promises have not materialized. According to the 1999 UN *Trade and Development Report,*

> The predicted gains to developing countries from the Uruguay Round [establishing the WTO] have proved to be exaggerated and, as feared, international capital movements have been particularly disruptive. Poverty and unemployment are again on the rise in developing countries which had struggled for many years to combat them. Income and welfare gaps between and within countries have widened further.[14]

Conflicts between Northern and Southern movements have been chronic, even when both have been critical of globalization from above. While Northern labor movements have strongly supported labor and environmental conditions in WTO rules, for example, those have been widely opposed not only by third world governments but by Southern NGOs such as the Third World Network, which has attacked them as a vehicle for Northern protectionism. Northern and Southern NGOs in Jubilee 2000 came into conflict over the so-called HIPC Initiative, which linked debt reduction with stringent structural adjustment–style conditionalities.[15] There has been similar division over the World Bank Inspection

Panel, to which local communities affected by Bank programs can appeal over the heads of their national governments.[16]

The American labor movement was widely criticized by third world NGOs for the way in which it opposed permanent normal trade relations (PNTR) for China. Walden Bello and Anuradha Mittal wrote,

> Organized labor is at the center of a motley coalition that is against granting PNTR to China.... This is not a progressive alliance but a right-wing populist alliance in the tradition of the anti-communist Big Government-Big Capital-Big Labor alliance during the Cold War, [and] the labor-capital alliance in the West that produced the Exclusion and Anti-Miscegenation Acts against Chinese, Japanese, and Filipino workers in the late 19th and early 20th centuries.[17]

Teamsters president James Hoffa could hardly have done more to drive a wedge between working people in the first and third worlds than when he told the National Press Club,

> What is going to happen in PNTR is that you're going to have a full employment program for people in China … [M]any, many people—our figures show a million people—are going to lose their jobs in this country because of PNTR.

Besides indicating that "a full employment program for China" was somehow something bad, Hoffa also managed to put a bigoted twist on the race to the bottom: "There's always somebody that will work cheaper. There's always some guy in a loincloth."[18]

Efforts to address such conflicts must start with a fundamental moral agreement that the present inequality of wealth and power is unconscionable and that the movement and all its parts must have as a central objective the elimination of third world poverty and ensuring third world peoples equal power in the shaping of the global future. Any movement that does not make such a commitment can be justly regarded as a vehicle for retaining existing privileges.

A continuing dialogue among Northern and Southern social movements is also a condition for addressing this conflict. Such a dialogue has been occurring for decades around UN forums, at the events surrounding IMF, World Bank, WTO, and similar global gatherings, and through networks and meetings sponsored by international NGOs and labor organizations. Some have had the specific objective of producing joint programs that include the concerns of Northern and Southern social movements.

For example, as the governments of the Western Hemisphere launched plans for a Free Trade Area of the Americas, trade unions, environmentalists, human rights organizations, and other NGOs launched an alternative Hemispheric Social Alliance. They met in Santiago, Chile, in 1998 and developed a proposal for "Social and Economic Alternatives to the Free Trade Area of the Americas."[19] It proposed "a set of fundamental principles and ideas which could underlie an alternative to the current form of globalization." Movements in both the North and the South need to incorporate ideas from such joint efforts in their own approaches.

Popular movements from the North and the South share many concrete objectives on which they can cooperate. For example, despite some disagreements, religious and other groups have been able to cooperate on a global campaign to cancel the debt of the world's poorest countries. People from first and third worlds worked side by side in Seattle to oppose a new round for the WTO; many reports indicate that third world WTO delegates were emboldened to resist first world demands by the people acting in the streets.[20] After major demonstrations in Washington, DC, in April 2000 against the IMF and World Bank, Walden Bello noted, "Finally people in the United States have woken up to the fact that these institutions are creating tremendous injustice and are willing to take to the streets in support of their brothers and sisters in the Third World."[21]

There is also a powerful common interest among Northern workers and the people of the South in resisting the austerity programs imposed on Southern countries by the IMF and the World Bank in the name of structural adjustment or as conditions for loans made in the wake of the Asian financial crisis. These conditions not only cut wages, healthcare, education, and environmental protection in poor countries; they also force countries such as South Korea, Brazil, and Russia to export steel and other manufactured goods to the United States at rock-bottom prices based on depression-level wages. A joint attack on structural adjustment–style policies, and support for growth driven by domestic demand in third world countries, could serve as the basis for a powerful alliance between first world labor and a wide range of forces in the third world.[22]

A group of international NGOs and union representatives has developed a common position opposing structural adjustment that is specifically intended as a means to unify civil society groups in the North and the South. It called for "South/North civil-society cooperation" to create "space in each country for the participatory development of and implementation of national economic policy through the effective functioning of democratic process and respect for labor and other internationally recognized human rights."[23] The AFL-CIO, which had lobbied for expanded IMF funding in 1998, took an unexpected step toward such an alliance by endorsing the April 16, 2000, legal demonstrations against the IMF and World Bank.

Beyond such specific campaigns, the tension between rich and poor countries requires a "grand bargain," initially developed among civil society groups, which integrates the needs of ordinary people in both into a common program.[24] Such a program must regard the present rich/poor divisions as unacceptable. It must make sustainable development in poor countries a central goal of the global economy, reversing the virtual debt peonage that globalization has imposed on most of the third world. At the same time, it must aim to restructure the economies of the rich countries to make them less destructive to the global environment. The elements of such a bargain have been worked out in the "Social and Economic Alternatives to the Free Trade Area of the Americas" document and other such joint North-South programs. While details vary somewhat, they generally include the following themes:

• Third world peoples and nations must be included in decision making about the future of the global economy. The process must move out of organizations like the IMF and G-7, which represent the rich countries. It requires, instead, a forum that picks up the dropped threads of the North-South Dialogue.[25]

• International trade rules should aim to help poor countries develop. They should favor a balance of internal market development and production for export. They should allow protection and subsidy of internal markets as long as they are part of sustainable development plans and not simply export subsidies or political favors. They should provide preferential access to rich countries' markets for poor countries' exports. They should encourage international commodity agreements to stabilize commodity prices and production levels.

• At the same time, global rules need to establish minimum human rights, labor, environmental, and social standards that apply to all countries, so that they are not forced to compete with each other by abusing their own people and environment.[26] These rules must not be a unilateral imposition by rich countries on poor ones. Indeed, they should particularly target the abuses in rich countries, such as denial of the right of workers to organize and strike, abuse of immigrant workers, and violation of the Rio agreements on protection of the environment. Their primary targets should not be countries, but rather corporations that violate the rules. The cost of conforming to these rules should be the responsibility of the world's rich, not the poor.

• International rules should permit developing countries to establish national policies supporting sustainable development. For example, governments should be allowed to establish performance requirements for foreign corporations, such as requirements for technology transfer, employment of local workers, and training of workers. They should be allowed to channel foreign capital to long-term investment in accord with a sustainable development plan. And they should be free to limit foreign and other private investment in industries that are critical for development.

• Resources should be deliberately transferred from the rich of the world to the poor. A starting point for this redistribution could be a so-called Tobin Tax on international financial transactions, with the proceeds devoted to investment in poor countries' development efforts.[27] A global investment fund should focus heavily on education, health, environmentally sound infrastructure, and job-creating programs in developing countries.

• Global policy must aim to promote poor countries' access to knowledge and technology. So-called intellectual property
rights must be subordinate to a right of access to the common
knowledge created by humanity.

Such a program will no doubt meet massive resistance from the
power nexus represented by the US Treasury Department, the global
corporations, and the international institutions they largely control.
But it corresponds to the interests of the world's people and to the
moral imperative to improve the conditions of the world's poor. It
also forms an essential part of a more general program to correct the
flaws of the global economy.

Some parts of this program, such as preferential market access
for third world products, might in themselves conflict with the interest of some first world workers. Other parts of the program, such
as requirements for labor and environmental protections, might
have costs for some in the third world. Yet each is part of an overall
program that will greatly benefit the great majority in both the South
and the North, in terms both of immediate economic interests and
of long-term environmental and social sustainability. And people in
the North and the South are far more likely to meet their own needs
in the context of a joint struggle for such a program.

Integrating the Links

Environmental/human need issues and North/South issues are
themselves closely linked. Both the so-called less developed countries (LDCs) of the third world and what perhaps should be called the
wrongly developed countries (WDCs) of the first world are in need
of radical change. While the former must develop in ways that are
environmentally sustainable, the latter are already environmentally
unsustainable; they need to dismantle those aspects of their economies that are wasteful and destructive and invest major resources in
rebuilding on an environmentally sound basis. (After all, it is the
WDCs that provide the lion's share of the world's pollution and
global warming gases.)[28]

Both tasks require large amounts of labor and resources. But
such an effort would provide more than enough employment for

people in all parts of the world. Such a form of sustainable development would provide full employment and greatly reduce the competition of workers against workers around the world.

It may be easier for people to ignore the concerns of others and simply focus on their own. But that is to put at risk the unity that is necessary for globalization from below to succeed. The agents of globalization from above will be more than happy to take advantage of unresolved divisions in the movement.

To resolve its contradictions, the movement for globalization from below needs a vision of the movement as a whole. It needs to construct common, integrative understandings, assimilate them into the perspective of each part of the movement, and use them to guide its action. And the movement needs to develop a common program for global transformation that articulates what those understandings mean in practice.

Chapter 5

A World to Win—for What?

As the era of globalization began to dawn, Margaret Thatcher is said to have coined the oft-quoted slogan that "there is no alternative" to neoliberal capitalism. Commenting on the Battle of Seattle, *Newsweek* wrote, "One of the most important lessons of Seattle is that there are now two visions of globalization on offer, one led by commerce, one by social activism."[1]

As we wrote in Chapter 2, "shared worldviews, paradigms, visions, frames, or ideologies" are a means to link groups with disparate traditions and experiences. They also provide a guide for efforts to transform the world, defining common values and norms and providing the basis for a common program.

While the critique of globalization from above is well developed, the emergence of the alternative vision is only in its early stages. The movement for globalization from below has no high priests authorized to proclaim its vision. The construction of that vision is an ongoing social process to which all movement participants can contribute—and as the poet William Blake wrote, "Would to God that all the Lord's people were prophets!"[2] Ultimately, participants will have to decide for themselves what version of that vision they consider valid. In this chapter, we review the emergence of that vision and suggest ways of putting it into the more concrete form of a common program.

What the Vision Is Not

To define the alternative vision, it is important first to understand what it is not:

• It is not a single vision, but rather a complex process in which many elements are converging, sometimes to form a new unity, at other times to jostle along side by side in the same direction. More important than any formulation of the vision that could be expressed in a manifesto is the fact that thousands of people all over the world are working at constructing that vision.

• It is not a universal faith, in effect a new world religion, with shared convictions about ultimate human meanings. The vision is shared by people from virtually every religion in the world and people with no religion at all.

• It is not a shared utopia. Images of the good society range from a realization of the positive aspects of modernity in a democratic, scientifically and technologically developed, ecologically sound, and socially just world order to a return to the life patterns of indigenous peoples, with many others in between.

• It is not a conventional political ideology like liberalism or Marxism with systematic conclusions drawn from agreed-to first principles.

• It is not a set of values or norms peculiar to the movement. The values and goals of globalization from below are the same as the rough global consensus articulated in innumerable UN documents, from the Universal Declaration of Human Rights to the most recent evaluations of environmental and social policy. Globalization from below is a movement *to implement* these widely shared global norms.[3]

• It is not an equivalent to the neoliberal program of globalization from above. While neoliberalism imposes one answer—the market—to every question, diversity is the essence of the alternative. The program of globalization from below is largely a means to allow people to develop democratically their own diverse and experimental approaches at local, regional, and national levels.

• The vision cannot be reduced to a set of reforms for fixing global economic institutions, although such reforms are a necessary part of its program. It differs from the various mainstream proposals for a "new architecture" for the global economy in at least two respects. It presupposes that the problems of globalization can only be corrected through a profound shift of wealth and power. And it asserts that the necessary changes will not be brought about by the purveyors of globalization from above, but rather by the united action of those challenging their power.

The Vision Process

The movement's vision reflects the diversity of situations and itineraries of its participants. Many of its elements originated in the distinct movements from which globalization from below originated but have been widely assimilated throughout the movement. For example, an emphasis on the need to protect the environment is now found not only among those who define themselves as environmentalists, but also among union activists and human rights advocates. Support for worker organizing to resist the race to the bottom is not limited to the labor movement. Desire to establish a culture that places more emphasis on nurturing and less on domination is common far beyond those whose primary identification is as feminists. Concern about third world poverty includes many who are not directly involved with issues of economic development.

Globalization from below remains rooted in a wide range of specific movements around specific concerns. But its unifying vision reframes these activities in ways that show their connection to the broader problems of globalization experienced by others. It interprets particular movements as responses to a common situation and as part of a common struggle.

For example, union organizing campaigns and campaigns for minimum and living wages at a local level can be redefined as part of the global resistance to the race to the bottom. Such minimum standards can be achieved both in civil society, through organizing and pressure campaigns, and by means of governmental regulation. These efforts also can involve defense of basic human rights, notably the rights to organize, bargain collectively, strike, and participate on an equal basis in the political process. Where organizing involves the struggles of groups that face discrimination, such as women and racial minorities, it also addresses another basic aspect of human rights and equality.

The process of creating a common vision for the movement must—and does—involve ongoing dialogue across the boundaries of countries and concerns. That dialogue has included the construction of transnational alternatives to NAFTA, the FTAA, and the MAI, as well as a vast range of movements that have addressed the problems of inequality, poverty, environment, and human rights at every level from local to global. Programmatic approaches must continue to evolve in the light of experience and as new needs and concerns emerge.

The roots of this vision process go beyond the movement itself. Some of them lie in an international discourse on human rights that goes back at least to the movement for the abolition of slavery. But it goes beyond the constricted concept that limits human rights to a few fixed political elements. It includes—in the spirit of the Universal Declaration of Human Rights—a full range not just of political but of economic, social, and cultural rights. It includes protection of the environment as a prerequisite to human rights and even human existence. It includes the rights of social groups, as well as of individuals.[4] And it envisions human rights as evolving with the emergence of new groups and concerns, as has happened so significantly with the rights of women, gays and lesbians, and indigenous peoples.[5]

Globalization from below also draws heavily on declarations that have been agreed to in and around UN conferences on the environment and development, women, human rights, social dimensions of development, and the like. These have gone a long way toward establishing a broad global consensus on what the world needs, one that is profoundly at odds with the realities of globalization from above.

The movement's vision is expressed in many forms. These include the demands and rationales of actions and campaigns; the programs presented by specific organizations; and the proposals of scholars and think tanks. Particularly important are joint statements that have been drawn up by coalitions whose members have had to take each others' approaches into account. The program proposals in the next chapter are based primarily upon such joint statements.

From Vision to Program

Sociologists speak of the "expressive function" of social movements. In the vernacular, this means that social movements let people vent. When movements do no more than allow people to vent their feelings, they may actually serve as a safety valve for the status quo, reducing pressure on the system.

Social change requires more than simply making a wish list that expresses one's values: wishing, for example, that nobody were poor, or that everybody would stop polluting. And social change requires more than fighting or even winning battles. It requires transforming relationships.

A program makes explicit the changes that a movement seeks to implement. It allows a movement to go beyond the expression of feeling to formulate its vision as a set of concrete changes that will realize its goals. A program mediates between aspirations and reality, transforming wishes into plans.

The movement that developed in response to globalization from above has tended to formulate its objectives in negative terms: block NAFTA, stop the MAI, end World Bank support for big dams, prevent a new round of the WTO. The very idea of developing a positive program sometimes meets resistance. Attention to such work can interrupt the expressive function, requiring a pause to reflect. In broad coalitions, it is easier to reach agreement on what you are against than on what you are for. Some fear that spelling out a program would add legitimacy to the schemes of those who merely wish to reform globalization from above to make it work more effectively. Forging a program requires taking into account the needs of others and the potential contradictions among one's own objectives. It involves a certain kind of abstraction from the immediate situation to envision possibilities that the movement does not currently have the power to realize. It also takes a degree of technical knowledge and some hard work.

The movement's actual aspirations go far beyond "just say no" to globalization. It is actually concerned with reversing the negative effects of globalization on poverty, the environment, human rights, and democracy. To do so, it is not enough just to halt globalization or block some of its institutions. The implicit goal of the movement is to solve the problems created or exacerbated by globalization. Articulating its positive objectives is a central aspect of moving from resistance to transformation.

Of course, a movement cannot be reduced to its program. A program is not a substitute for concrete struggles. The best program in the world means little if it is merely "nowhere plans for nobody," unconnected to people determined to implement it. Wonkism is no substitute for movement spirit, "for the letter killeth, but the spirit giveth life." A program must be more than a laundry list of the proposals of various constituencies. Rather, it should be an integrated set of changes in the social framework that meet both the common and the distinct needs of those affected. It thereby constructs a common interest that incorporates the particular interests of different groups. This allows currently incompatible needs—for example, between jobs and environment—to become compatible.[6]

A program needs to address both what can be accomplished today and how the movement would use the far greater power it hopes to have in the future. It includes what people can accomplish right now through their own action in civil society.[7] It includes what they can currently impose on established institutions through struggle. And it includes the changes they will make should the balance of forces shift in their favor. A program specifies norms that the movement aims to impose on corporations, markets, states, international institutions, and other power centers. They can then be held accountable to those norms, initially through campaigns to change particular practices, ultimately through enforceable rules.

A program needs to perform four basic functions in relation to diverse elements within the movement, the wider public, the opposition, and the world to be changed. First, it must unify the concerns and approaches of different parts of the movement. Second, it should appeal to the uncommitted for their support. Third, it needs to help fragment, neutralize, delegitimate, or even win over parts of the opposition. Finally, it must propose good solutions to the problems of the real world.

In the next chapter, we propose a draft of such a program.

Chapter 6

Draft of a Global Program

We wrote in Chapter 1 that participants in the movement for globalization from below have varied goals, but the movement's unifying goal is "to bring about sufficient democratic control over states, markets, and corporations to permit people and the planet to survive and begin to shape a viable future." In this chapter we present the draft of a program to impose such democratic control. It proposes institutions and practices designed to turn global norms into enforceable rules.

This draft program is offered as a contribution to the ongoing process of constructing a program for globalization from below. It is not derived from an underlying political philosophy, but rather is synthesized from the solutions that diverse constituencies have proposed on their itineraries to globalization from below. It represents a work in progress, based on elements that have been percolating through the movement. Similar approaches have been formulated in previous programs presented by transnational groupings of various kinds.[1] Many of these elements have been included in the Global Sustainable Development Resolution cosponsored by a group of progressive members of the US Congress.[2]

This synthesis is guided by Chapter 1's analysis of the conflict between globalization from above and globalization from below; Chapter 2's concept of social movements imposing norms; Chapter 3's emphasis on addressing the different levels from the local to the global; Chapter 4's approach to integrating the needs of people and nature and of North and South; and Chapter 5's delineation of the origins and functions of a program.

This program is not the design for a utopia or a plan to fix all the world's ills. Its purpose is to provide a win-win framework for the many constituencies converging into globalization from below. It seeks ways that their needs, concerns, and interests can be complementary rather than contradictory.[3] Rather than treating trade, finance, development, labor, environment, agriculture, and other aspects of globalization as separate, unrelated compartments, this draft program addresses the global economy holistically. While each element also requires detailed elaboration, all are presented here as parts of an integrated project.

While this program aims to change the global economy, it is designed to be fought for and implemented as much in local arenas as in Washington or Geneva. For example, local struggles over the right to organize unions and control over corporate waste disposal can help level labor and environmental conditions upward, especially if they receive solidarity support from a broad coalition around the world. Reducing the volatility of the global economy involves local economic development protected from the gyrations of the global casino. While this program ultimately envisions new rules and institutions for the global economy, many of its objectives can be implemented piecemeal through pressure on particular corporations, governments, and institutions.

The goals of globalization from below are often expressed in broad language advocating just and sustainable development. One formulation describes the movement's goal as "a new economy based on fairness and justice, on a sound ecology and a healthy environment, one that protects human rights and serves freedom."[4] Another calls for a "sustainable, socially just and democratically accountable" system.[5] Our sketch of a program for globalization from below is organized around seven basic principles:

1. Level labor, environmental, social, and human rights conditions upward.

2. Democratize institutions at every level from local to global.

3. Make decisions as close as possible to those they affect.

4. Equalize global wealth and power.

5. Convert the global economy to environmental sustainability.

6. Create prosperity by meeting human and environmental needs.

7. Protect against global boom and bust.

1. Level labor, environmental, social, and human rights conditions upward.

Globalization from above is creating a race to the bottom, an economic war of all against all in which each workforce, community, and country is forced to compete by offering lower labor, social, environmental, and human rights conditions. The result is impoverishment, inequality, volatility, degradation of democracy, and environmental destruction. Halting the race to the bottom requires raising labor, environmental, social, and human rights conditions for those at the bottom. Such upward leveling can start with specific struggles to raise conditions for those who are being driven downward. Ultimately, minimum environmental, labor, social, and human rights standards must be incorporated in national and international law. Such standards protect communities and countries from the pressure to compete by sacrificing their rights and environment. Rising conditions for those at the bottom can also expand employment and markets and generate a virtuous circle of economic growth.

Raise labor, environmental, social, and human rights conditions locally: The fight to reverse the race to the bottom can begin at home. For example, living wage campaigns in local communities can be part of the process of upward leveling for wages. Organizing unions, ensuring the right to organize, establishing rights for workers in contingent jobs, and creating an adequate social safety net all establish rights and raise standards for those threatened by the downward pressures of the global economy. Campaigns for environmental justice and the protection of local environments similarly resist the environmental race to the bottom.[6]

Force standards on corporations: Workers and other citizens, acting in civil society, should pressure global corporations to negotiate minimum global standards for labor and environment.[7] National governments should be pressured to incorporate such standards in national trade laws and international financial and trade organizations.

Incorporate global standards in national law: Internationally recognized labor rights are regularly violated not only in the third world but also in the US. Every country's law should enforce those rights at home and require their corporations to meet international labor standards throughout the world.

Put floors, not ceilings, in international trade agreements: NAFTA, the WTO, and other trade agreements often forbid labor, environmental, health, and other regulations that exceed the agreement's own standards. Such ceilings should be eliminated to allow communities and countries to set their own minimum standards.

Negotiate agreements to protect minimum standards for labor, environment, and human rights: Such agreements can be implemented by established institutions such as international trade organizations or the UN, or by new ones established for the purpose.[8]

2. Democratize institutions at every level from local to global.

Globalization from above has restricted the power of self-government for people all over the world. At the heart of globalization from below lies democratization—making institutions accountable to those they affect.

Open the dialogue on the future of the global economy to all: The movement has already initiated a participatory global dialogue on democratizing the global economy. That dialogue should be expanded in every local community, in every country, and worldwide. A model here is the movement in Canada, which organized community forums across the country to discuss a people's alternative to the MAI.[9]

Establish a Global Economy Truth Commission: Globalization has been conducted behind the back of the world's people. A truth commission can provide citizens of the world with the information they need to monitor the results, impacts, and failures of economic institutions and policy at every level. The Truth Commission's inquest should be given the powers to investigate, publicize, and refer abuses in the use of international funds and the powers of international financial institutions to other authorities.

Democratize international trade and financial institutions: It is unacceptable that a few rich countries monopolize decision making regarding the global economy's future through their control of the IMF, World Bank, and WTO and through the control of major policy decisions by the G-7. Voting in international financial and trade institutions must move toward the standard of equal representation for the world's people.[10] International economic policy making must move from the rich men's club of the G-7 to forums where poor countries are fairly represented. International economic institutions must be made transparent in all their operations.

Let those affected by international economic policies participate in making them: Instead of closed negotiations with top government and corporate officials, decisions about international economic agreements and loans should require participation by labor unions, environmental groups, women's organizations, development organizations, and other major sectors of civil society in each country.

Establish an enforceable code of conduct for global corporations: Corporations that operate in more than one country should be subject to a global code of conduct with minimum requirements for disclosure of activities and compliance with labor and environmental standards. The UN Center on Transnational Corporations was in the process of developing such a code, but it was stopped by US opposition.[11]

Make corporations legally accountable: Corporations should be held legally liable for harms caused abroad and be subject to actions for relief in home-country courts. They should be required to disclose their use, emission, and accidental discharge of toxic substances and the names and addresses of their fully or partially owned facilities, contractors, and subcontractors.

End the domination of politics by big money: Ending "crony capitalism" means reducing the domination of political systems and media by economic oligarchs and increasing the capacity of people to organize themselves at the grassroots. This is as necessary in the United States as in Indonesia, Mexico, or Russia.[12]

3. Make decisions as close as possible to those they affect.

The movement for globalization from below should aim to construct a multilevel global economy. In accordance with the subsidiarity principle, power and initiative should be concentrated at as low a level as possible, with higher-level regulation established where and only where necessary. This approach envisions relatively self-reliant, self-governing communities, states, provinces, countries, and regions, with global regulation only sufficient to protect the environment, redistribute resources, block the race to the bottom, and perform other essential functions.

Build a community-controlled economic sector: A key strategy for protecting local communities from the vagaries of the global economy is to create an economic sector that is partially insulated from global markets. This sector needs to be rooted in and controlled by local people and based on meeting local needs. Creating such a sector involves initiating local projects, such as worker and community-owned businesses, cooperatives, development banks, and loan funds. It also involves supportive public policies, such as government procurement and funding policies that support sustainable local development.

Make corporations locally accountable: Local labor unions, community groups, and governments should pressure corporations to negotiate with them regarding acceptable norms of behavior.

Establish local control of local environments: In accord with the principle of subsidiarity, any activity with potential impact on the local environment should require the informed consent of the people in that community.[13]

Protect local and national economic development capacity: Current trade agreements often interfere with the right of countries and communities to pursue local economic development objectives, such as job creation and targeting development for needy groups. International agreements should instead protect that right.

Establish regional "no raiding" pacts: States and provinces should agree not to compete to provide subsidies to lure companies to relocate. No-raiding rules exist in the EU, and corporations have been heavily fined for taking state and provincial subsidies to relocate. Unions in the northeastern US have proposed a multistate agreement that would block the regional race to the bottom by punishing companies that relocate to areas with lower standards.[14]

4. Equalize global wealth and power.

The current gap between the global rich and poor is unacceptable; it is unconscionable to act as if it can be a permanent feature of the global economy. It is equally unacceptable to assume that the rich countries of the world can call all the shots regarding the global economy's future. Policy at every level should prioritize economic advancement of the most oppressed and exploited people, including women, immigrants, racial and ethnic minorities, and indigenous peoples. It should increase power, capability, resources, and income for those at the bottom.

Shop and invest ethically: Individual consumers, institutions, and governments should use their buying power to purchase goods, services, and investments that support acceptable labor, environmental, and social conditions. Consumer power is already being used in such areas as the boycott of companies that invest in Burma and of World Bank bonds. Consumer purchasing power is also being harnessed to support fair trade—for example, through the Rugmark consumer seal for rugs produced without child labor; the creation of organizations to certify that garments and other products are not produced under sweatshop conditions; and the marketing of crafts and coffee from fairly paid workers and employee-owned cooperatives.

Revive the North-South Dialogue: In the 1970s, the rich and poor countries of the world initiated the North-South Dialogue, a series of ongoing UN discussions designed to establish a New International Economic Order that would support third world development. This dialogue, terminated by Ronald Reagan, should be revived as a step toward providing poor countries with a greater voice in global policies.

End global debt slavery: Today poor countries are forced to run their economies to pay debts promoted by foreign investors and taken on by corrupt governments that did not represent their people. The wealthy countries and the international financial institutions should immediately cancel the debts of the poorest countries. Repayment requirements should be limited for all underdeveloped countries.[15] No poor country should be required to use more than a small proportion of its income for debt repayment.

Make global markets work for developing economies: Rather than promoting indiscriminate free trade, trade policy should specifically encourage development of poor countries by providing them with preferential access to first world markets. (This is already done in a modest way with the Generalized System of Preferences, which reduces tariffs for developing countries.) To reverse the fall in commodity prices that has devastated third world producers and to prevent a global race to the bottom in commodities, commodity agreements to promote stability in price and production levels should be encouraged.

Provide developing countries access to technical knowledge: International trade agreements have enormously expanded the so-called intellectual property rights of corporations. This blocks poor countries from the knowledge they need to develop and become more self-reliant. Often this causes terrible hardship, such as the murderous drug company policy of using their "intellectual property rights" to price lifesaving drugs out of reach of the world's ordinary citizens. Global policy should encourage rapid and inexpensive access to all forms of technical knowledge to aid sustainable development. Those with access to such knowledge should, when necessary, commit "intellectual civil disobedience" by helping make it available to those who need it.

Invest in sustainable development: Global investment should be redirected from private financial speculation to one or more public international investment funds. The primary purpose of these funds should be to meet human and environmental needs by channeling money into locally controlled, environmentally sustainable, long-term investment. Sources for funding could include a Tobin Tax on international currency transactions; a global tax on carbon use designed to reduce greenhouse gas emissions; reductions in military spending; and public and private investment.[16] Such funds could also counter global economic cycles by appropriate expansion and contraction of their activities.

5. Convert the global economy to environmental sustainability.

The world is in the midst of a global environmental catastrophe. Ill-conceived economic activity is disrupting the basic balances of climate and ecology on which human life depends. Globalization is rapidly accelerating that ongoing catastrophe. The sources of environmental destruction lie primarily in the wrongly developed countries of the North and in the activities of global corporations in the South. The only way to reverse this catastrophe is to halt the present dynamic of globalization and meet human needs by technologies and social practices that progressively reduce the negative impact of the economy on the environment.

Transform the production and consumption patterns of wrongly developed countries: The so-called developed or industrialized countries of the North produce the lion's share of the world's pollution and climate-changing carbon emissions. The technological and social means to change their destructive patterns exist but are not being utilized. Public policy, including taxation, regulation, planning, and investment, must be directed to completely rebuilding these wrongly developed economies on an environmentally sustainable basis.

Make international environmental agreements enforceable: International agreements have been developed to combat global warming, protect endangered species, and restrict foreign dumping of toxic waste. But these agreements have little provision for enforcement. For example, many countries have ignored the agreements they signed at the Rio conference on environment and development. Such agreements should now be made enforceable by incorporating sanctions like those for protection of international property rights in the WTO.[17]

Incorporate environmental protections in trade agreements: The WTO, NAFTA, and other trade agreements should discourage environmentally destructive practices. Countries should be free to ban import of goods produced under conditions that violate environmental principles.

End the despoiling of natural resources for export: Countries should not be required by the IMF, World Bank, or global investors to chop down their forests, overfarm their lands, and overfish their waters to service their debts or increase investor profit.

Encourage sustainable development: Establish sustainable development plans at local and national levels. Pursue "conservation-based development" that combines good jobs and income with environmental enhancement. Focus international aid on helping to implement sustainable development plans.

6. Create prosperity by meeting human and environmental needs.

Today, an estimated 1 billion people are unemployed. Millions are forced to leave rural areas and migrate to cities or around the world seeking work. Meanwhile, the world's vast need for goods and services to alleviate poverty and to reconstruct society on an environmentally sustainable basis goes unmet. A goal of economic policy at every level must be to create a new kind of full employment based on meeting those needs.

Encourage development, not austerity: Neoliberalism, the IMF, and the World Bank have imposed austerity policies on much of the world, leading to massive unemployment and the destruction of small businesses and farms. Instead, local, national, and global policies should aim to ensure livable wages. They should make credit available for small and medium-sized locally owned businesses and farms. They should pursue a progressive tax policy that reduces the burden on the poor. This will help reverse the destructive competition that is promoted by globalization from above.

Promote local food production for local needs: Today's global economy subsidizes corporate food exports while forcing countries to open up to foreign food imports, thereby driving millions of small-scale farmers off the land. Instead, global policy should promote small-scale, environmentally sound farming for local markets. It should end agricultural export dumping. It should encourage countries to provide basic food security for their people.[18]

Utilize development planning techniques: Governments should revive the development planning techniques that have been forbidden by neoliberalism and its institutions. Such tools include reserving some economic sectors for public, state, or national ownership. They also include performance requirements designed to achieve local, regional, or national economic objectives, such as requirements for local inputs and local hiring preferences.

Promote long-term investment: Short-term foreign investment that just skims off speculative profits does little or nothing for economic development. Only long-term investment that builds economic capacity and protects the environment is likely to benefit poorer countries. Public policy should encourage investment that leads to genuine sustainable development, not exploitation of people and resources for short-term gain.

Reestablish national full employment policies: Neoliberal economic policies have used mass unemployment to keep wages low, allegedly to fight inflation. National governments should instead use tax, budget, and monetary policies to ensure full employment.

7. Protect against global boom and bust.

The era of globalization has been an era of volatility. Its repeated crises have destroyed local and national economies overnight and driven hundreds of millions of people into poverty. An unregulated global economy has led to huge flows of speculative funds that can swamp national economies. No one country can control these forces on its own. Yet neoliberal economics and the major economic powers have resisted any changes that might restrict the freedom of capital. Economic security for ordinary people requires just such restrictions.

Utilize capital controls: Under the articles of the IMF, countries have the power to impose controls on the movement of capital across their borders. This power, which was used regularly by most countries for many decades, helps protect against wild rushes of money into and out of a country. But the current policies of the IMF and other institutions and the pressures of globalization have largely undermined the capacity of individual countries to use such controls effectively. Countries and international institutions should cooperate to restore their effectiveness.

Establish a "hot money" tax: A global tax on short-term hot money transactions—known as a Tobin Tax—will reduce global speculation, as well as provide resources for world development and environmental protection.

Coordinate demand in the major economies: The maintenance of prosperity worldwide requires cooperation of the major economic powers working in parallel to ensure demand adequate to help all economies grow.[19]

Assure global liquidity: Financial crises have been a regular part of globalization. When such crises occur, short-term lack of liquidity can cause long-term economic devastation. Provisions should be made in advance to reduce the effects of such liquidity crises, especially on poorer countries. In the 1970s, for example, a system of Special Drawing Rights was established to protect the global economy from liquidity squeezes. The expansion of this or an equivalent system is required today.

Stabilize exchange rates: An effective system to prevent wild fluctuations in currency exchange rates existed for decades under the original design of the Bretton Woods agreement, but it was abandoned in the early 1970s. Such a system should be revived through international cooperation. It should aim to help countries adjust to changing conditions without drastic devaluations and massive increases in exports.[20]

Make speculators pay for their losses: International bailouts have insulated large banks and investors from the consequences of their high-risk speculations. This leads to what economists call moral hazard—encouraging more such speculative ventures. The result is even more international volatility. Assistance provided for economies in trouble must go to benefit the people, not to line the pockets of the international investors who lured them into trouble in the first place.

Establish a permanent insolvency mechanism for indebted countries: Such a mechanism can draw on the experience of other bankruptcy procedures for governments, such as the municipal insolvency provisions of Chapter 9 of US bankruptcy law. Arbitration panels should represent both debtors and creditors, and should establish the debtor country's capacity to pay, taking into account necessary expenditures for social safety nets to protect a minimum of human dignity of the poor and the debtor's economic future.[21]

Develop international monetary regulation: Over the course of centuries, nations developed central banks to regulate private banks, control the supply of money, and counter booms and busts. But globalization has undermined their capacity to do so, creating a global monetary system that is wildly out of control. That makes it necessary to develop international institutions to perform or assist with functions of monetary regulation currently performed inadequately by national central banks. Regulating global banks, for example, requires international cooperation. Equally important, the non-bank financial services companies that have grown explosively in the past decades need to be brought under national and international regulation. And, since money has become global, an international equivalent to the national regulation of interest rates and money supply is needed.[22] Such regulation must support basic objectives of just and sustainable development.

•

The movement for globalization from below is indeed developing an alternative vision for the global economy. It is not just a nostalgic desire to return to the past, nor a fearful rejection of a wider world, nor a laundry list of wishes and hopes. It is a program for the transformation of the global economy. Its elements are concrete enough to implement. They fit together well enough to be synergistic. They address the needs of the overwhelming majority of the world's people.

People can begin to implement these elements wherever and whenever they have the power to do so. As some elements are implemented, that can help strengthen the capacity to implement others.

That doesn't mean that the program presented here is adequate or final. On the contrary, it represents only an early attempt to put the proposals of different parts of the movement together into a common whole. The next step is to review this and other such syntheses in the light of the problems and concerns of different constituencies and to revise the whole in the light of the various needs to which it must respond. That is a work for many hands.

Chapter 7

Self-Organization from Below

The NGO Swarm

As the era of globalization dawned, many social activists saw organizing globally as an insurmountable problem. Organizations and their constituencies were overwhelmingly national. Even those that purported to be international were often national organizations weakly linked at the very top by a figurehead leadership and an occasional international conference.

The movement for globalization from below, it turned out, required not a more centralized global structure but rather global self-organization from below. In fact, new forms of organization have emerged to make global linking possible. They are not the brainchild of some organizational genius but rather the work of many hands responding to the new situation. This emerging form of organization is often referred to by such terms as international civil society, NGOs, or international advocacy networks.[1]

Future historians will no doubt study an extraordinary article in *The Economist* that recounted the rise of the new form that became so visible in Seattle.

The non-governmental organizations (NGOs) that descended on Seattle were a model of everything the trade negotiators were not. They were well organized. They built unusual coalitions (environmentalists and labour groups, for instance, bridged old gulfs to jeer the WTO together). They had a clear agenda to derail the talks. And they were masterly users of the media.[2]

But, *The Economist* pointed out, the Battle of Seattle is only the latest in a string of NGO victories.

> The watershed was the Earth Summit in Rio de Janeiro in 1992, when the NGOs roused enough public pressure to push through agreements on controlling greenhouse gases. In 1994, protesters dominated the World Bank's anniversary meeting with a "Fifty Years Is Enough" campaign, and forced a rethink of the Bank's goals and methods. In 1998, an ad hoc coalition of consumer-rights activists and environmentalists helped to sink the Multilateral Agreement on Investment (MAI), a draft treaty to harmonize rules on foreign investment under the aegis of the OECD. In the past couple of years another global coalition of NGOs, Jubilee 2000, has pushed successfully for a dramatic reduction in the debts of the poorest countries.

Further, the NGO agenda is not confined to economic issues.

> One of the biggest successes of the 1990s was the campaign to outlaw landmines, where hundreds of NGOs, in concert with the Canadian government, pushed through a ban in a year. Nor is it confined to government agendas. Nike has been targeted for poor labour conditions in its overseas factories, Nestle for the sale of powdered baby milk in poor countries, Monsanto for genetically modified food.... In short, citizens' groups are increasingly powerful at the corporate, national and international level.

Although such organizations date back at least to the international campaign for the abolition of slavery, the social and economic conditions of the past decade have led them to proliferate.

> The end of communism, the spread of democracy in poor countries, technological change and economic integration, globalization, in short, have created fertile soil for the rise of NGOs. Globalization itself has exacerbated a host of worries: over the environment, labour rights, human rights, consumer rights and so on. Democratisation and technological progress have revolutionized the way in which citizens can unite to express their disquiet.

New technology has helped.

When groups could communicate only by telephone, fax, or mail, it was prohibitively expensive to share information or build links between different organizations. Now information can be dispersed quickly, and to great effect, online. The MAI was already in trouble when a draft of the text, posted on the Internet by an NGO, allowed hundreds of hostile watchdog groups to mobilise against it. Similarly, the Seattle trade summit was disrupted by dozens of websites which alerted everyone (except, it seems, the Seattle police), to the protests that were planned.

New coalitions can be built on line. Much of the pre-Seattle coalition building between environmental and citizens' groups, for instance, was done by e-mail. About 1,500 NGOs signed an anti-WTO declaration set up on line by Public Citizen, a consumer-rights group. That, acknowledges Mike Dolan, a leading organiser of the protest, would have been impossible without e-mail. More important, the Internet allows new partnerships between groups in rich and poor countries. Armed with compromising evidence of local labour practices or environmental degradation from southern NGOs, for example, activists in developed countries can attack corporations much more effectively.

This phenomenon, amorphous groups of NGOs, linked online, descending on a target has been dubbed an 'NGO swarm' in a RAND study by David Ronfeldt and John Arguilla. And such groups are awful for governments to deal with. An NGO swarm, say the RAND researchers, has no central leadership or command structure; it is multi-headed, impossible to decapitate. And it can sting a victim to death.

The Network Structure

The essence of the new organizational form is not simply the NGO per se, but what political scientists Margaret Keck and Kathryn Sikkink call "advocacy networks." They define networks as "forms of organization characterized by voluntary, reciprocal and horizontal patterns of communication and exchange."[3] These networks may include not only conventional NGOs, but also local social movements, foundations, the media, churches, trade unions, consumer organizations, intellectuals, parts of regional and international intergovernmental organizations, and parts of the executive and/or parliamentary branches of governments.[4]

Such networks exchange information and support a dense nexus of communication among participants. They also develop a common language and frame issues for participants and the public.[5] Indeed, networks are defined primarily by their frames. Individuals and groups generally participate in a network to the extent that they accept its central frame.

Networks have become the main vehicle through which the campaigns of globalization from below have been organized. They function differently in campaigns than either conventional organizations or coalitions. There may be a lead organization and perhaps a formal coalition of supporters, but in practice most transnational campaigns emerge from planning within networks and are conducted by them, often across formal organizational lines. They are marked by what might be called cross-organization team leadership.[6]

Network participants can be highly diverse and may disagree on many matters, as long as they accept the network's defining frame of the issues that it addresses. Individuals can participate in them directly, whether or not they are formally affiliated through organizations. Segments of organizations can participate in them, and in the actions they launch, while other segments remain apart.

From the Net to the Street

A striking parallel to the NGO network is the form of organization developed for the Battle of Seattle and other major confrontations with the powers and principalities of globalization from above. Starhawk, an activist from the San Francisco Bay Area, describes "How We Really Shut Down the WTO":

> When authoritarians think about leadership, the picture in their minds is of one person, usually a guy, or a small group standing up and telling other people what to do. Power is centralized and requires obedience.
>
> In contrast, our model of power was decentralized, and leadership was invested in the group as a whole. People were empowered to make their own decisions, and the centralized structures

were for co-ordination, not control....

The participants in the action were organized into small groups called Affinity Groups. Each group was empowered to make its own decisions around how it would participate in the blockade....

Affinity groups were organized into clusters. The area around the Convention Center was broken down into thirteen sections, and affinity groups and clusters committed to hold particular sections. As well, some groups were "flying groups"—free to move to wherever they were most needed. All of this was co-ordinated at Spokescouncil meetings, where Affinity Groups each sent a representative who was empowered to speak for the group....

When faced with tear gas, pepper spray, rubber bullets and horses, groups and individuals could assess their own ability to withstand the brutality. As a result, blockade lines held in the face of incredible police violence.... No centralized leader could have co-ordinated the scene in the midst of the chaos, and none was needed—the organic, autonomous organization we had proved far more powerful and effective....

The affinity groups, clusters, spokescouncils and working groups involved with DAN [the Direct Action Network] made decisions by consensus—a process that allows every voice to be heard and that stresses respect for minority opinions. Consensus was part of the nonviolence and jail trainings and we made a small attempt to also offer some special training in meeting facilitation. We did not interpret consensus to mean unanimity. The only mandatory agreement was to act within the nonviolent guidelines. Beyond that, the DAN organizers set a tone that valued autonomy and freedom over conformity, and stressed co-ordination rather than pressure to conform.

The action included art, dance, celebration, song, ritual and magic. It was more than a protest; it was an uprising of a vision of true abundance, a celebration of life and creativity and connection, that remained joyful in the face of brutality and brought alive the creative forces that can truly counter those of injustice and control.[7]

Organizational Strengths

What is being created is a coordinated social movement composed of relatively autonomous groupings. It is a structure that differs from either an interest group pressuring the government or a party contesting for state power. It eschews a sharp distinction between organizers and the rank and file.

This network structure has proved itself well suited to the needs of globalization from below. It has been able to forge cooperation among diverse constituencies all over the world. Its fluidity is adapted to today's high velocity of change.[8]

The network form superbly fulfills many of the movement functions defined in Chapter 2. It makes it easy for people who are beginning to have doubts about the status quo to join together. It can organize withdrawal of consent in a great variety of forms. It is highly flexible in linking a variety of groups at many different levels.

The network form is also resistant to some of the common pitfalls to which social movements are prone described in Chapter 2. It is difficult to monopolize the flow of communication within networks or to block its flow across organizational boundaries. Networks are resistant to leadership domination; their leaders are largely dependent on persuasion, rather than on control of scarce organizational resources or on some form of muscle. (So far, the movement for globalization from below has developed respected, but not charismatic, let alone authoritarian, leaders.) When authority is delegated, it quickly expires, and is only renewed in the presence of active trust. Networks appear to be far more resistant to sectarian takeover than more conventional organizational forms. Such a decentralized form also allows experimentation, which means that failures are less likely to be catastrophic for the movement as a whole.

Organizational Weaknesses

The rise of networks reflects a decline in the importance of traditional forms of organization, which in turn reflects to some extent the individualism and fragmentation of contemporary life. When thousands of people lived in the same neighborhoods, worked long-term in the same workplaces as their neighbors, and shared the same culture, it was natural for them to see a common interest and belong to the same unions, political parties, and other organizations. Networks reflect the breakdown of this kind of community uniformity, as well as an effort to develop forms of collectivity that are viable in a more fragmented society.

Networks require a high level of personal responsibility compared to conventional organizations. It is both a vice and a virtue that this form does not permit one to meet one's obligations by sending an annual contribution or dues check.

NGOs and networks by no means eliminate inequality. Where access to such resources as foundations, contributors, training, research support, media attention, and social prestige are unequal, networks, like other structures, tend to reproduce those inequalities. They certainly have not eliminated power differentials between the North and the South or between women and men, for example.

In contrast to an organization, a network has no formal mechanism for resolving internal conflict. Intra-NGO and intra-network struggle has not been unusual. For example, there has been very visible conflict between the Northern and Southern wings of Jubilee 2000. The planning for the Battle of Seattle and other major demonstrations has also involved significant conflict. With no one authorized to make decisions for the movement as a whole, negotiation provides the only vehicle for addressing such disputes.[9]

Networks and affinity-group councils have no formal means to control or differentiate themselves from groups that would deliberately disrupt their activities. In Seattle, a few dozen people who trashed a few stores captured massive media attention and reshaped the public perception of the actions of tens of thousands of nonviolent protestors. A major joint demonstration between environmentalists and trade unionists in early 2000 was called off over the question of how to deal with the possibility of such disruptions.

NGOs can function as a new elite.[10] They possess technical expertise, organization, and funding, and they dispense major resources. NGOs now deliver more aid than the whole UN system.[11]

NGOs can also serve as cover for privatization of public functions. They are vulnerable, as Frieder Otto Wolf puts it, to "serving as a vehicle for political irresponsibility" by allowing responsibilities of governments to be "outsourced" to NGOs.[12]

NGOs can be created or captured by elite interests and serve as their agents. Such "coopted NGOs" (CONGOs) can undermine movement efforts. Examples include the "wise use" environmental groups, NGOs that receive their funding and take their policy cues from national governments or international organizations, and the church group in a poor Washington, DC, neighborhood that was paid in late 1999 to hold a demonstration supporting genetically engineered food. A particularly crude example was the self-described "grassroots group" called the Mobilization for Negotiation that was formed shortly before major demonstrations in Washington, DC, against the IMF and World Bank; it denounced the demonstrations' organizers as invoking "1960's demonstration nostalgia to entice and entangle youngsters in destructive protests" and announced that it had scheduled a meeting with officials of the World Bank.[13]

The network form presents problems of representation: an organization representing one person can appear as the equivalent of an organization representing 10,000 people.

Finally, there is the broad problem of accountability. Clearly, a government dominated by private corporate interests or an authoritarian political party cannot be regarded as the sole legitimate representative of its people. But what about movements, NGOs, or networks? They claim to speak for unrepresented people, but they are always vulnerable to the charge of being "self-appointed representatives" with no legitimate right to speak for anyone but themselves.

Ultimately there is no solution to this problem other than the reconstitution of genuinely representative institutions. But social movements can't wait for that, especially since they are among the prime vehicles by which such democratization can be promoted. What movements must do—and generally try to do—is to win public support by making themselves genuinely representative of the needs and interests of their constituents and of society. If they succeed, most people will support what the movement does, even though it has not been formally authorized to do it.

Networks and the Movement As a Whole

A social movement rarely takes the form of a single organization. Often what looks like a single movement from one perspective appears as a collection of interacting movements and organizations from another. It is rare to find a movement that does not contain elements of conflict within it. A social movement can nonetheless be grasped as an entity because all its elements are interacting and together form more than the sum of the parts.

How does a network of networks function in practice? Typically, particular NGOs take continuing responsibility for particular issues and social spheres. One may focus on the problem of large dams, another on human rights in a particular country, a third on the sweatshops of a particular corporation. These organizations hold "fixed fronts," so to speak, keeping a constant watch on the arenas and actors of their concern. However, the network structure allows large amounts of human and even material resources to flow rapidly to a particularly active front, allowing "concentrated forces" of "ready reserves" when they are needed. People can similarly move back and forth between big events like the Battle of Seattle and their daily struggles and responsibilities in particular localities and sectors.

The surprising level of unity that has marked the movement for globalization from below has been achieved without centralized organization, either nationally or globally. It is composed primarily of locally and nationally based issue groups, transnational linking organizations, and extensive networking conducted via the Internet. It seems unlikely that such a diverse global movement could ever develop a centralized organization and leadership. Unity will have to be maintained and deepened by other means.

The strongest force for unity is the pressure of rank-and-file activists who understand and want it. The Internet allows them to network across organization lines and to pressure leaders and organizations to remain unified.

Some Next Steps for Organizational Development

There are several initiatives which, while in keeping with the overall network form, would further adapt it to the needs of globalization from below as a whole:

- Creating venues in which to debate and sort out long-range objectives in ways that are insulated from immediate tactical decisions so that short-term tactical needs don't determine the way in which long-term objectives are defined. Such discussions must include representation of all of those who will ultimately be needed to achieve the movement's objectives.

- Establishing vehicles for self-critical reflection on the movement by its participants.

- Strengthening of linking organizations whose function is to build unity among different parts of the movement.

- Developing means to grant and withhold legitimacy from people acting as representatives of the movement in specific contexts, such as organizing events, presenting positions to the public, or negotiating with representatives of other forces and institutions.

- Opening avenues to allow new groups of people to link with and participate in the movement on terms that are acceptable to them.

- Establishing means to let grassroots groups around the world make direct links less mediated by NGOs, for example, by ensuring Internet access and training to impoverished groups.

- Developing ways to link internationally the big protest movements represented by national general and mass strikes.

- Establishing an annual day and week for coordinated events all over the world to show the global movement for globalization from below, in all its diversity, to itself and to the world.[14]

Chapter 8

No Movement Is an Island

The overall balance of social forces will not be solely determined by globalization from above and globalization from below. It will also depend on the broad configuration of social alliances that each constructs and on forces independent of either.

Advocates of globalization from below need to maintain their crucial role as an independent global opposition. At the same time, they need to recognize that this movement is only one of many actors that will play a role in shaping the future. Positive outcomes will depend not only on the movement itself, but also on the development of many other forces. The movement can often influence that development.

The movement for globalization from below needs to encourage forces outside itself to engage in resistance to the negative aspects of globalization, support efforts for change, and organize their own alternatives—and it needs to do so in ways that do not undermine its own independent role. At the same time, it needs to weaken and divide its opponents, something that can often be done best not by frontal attack but by jujitsu tactics that emphasize issues that are divisive and/or contradictory for the opposition.

This chapter considers how the movement relates to allies, the public, the right, the electoral arena, regionalism, and efforts at reform from above. While similar issues arise all over the world, most of this chapter focuses on the United States.

Allies

There are many organized groups whose interests conflict at some points with globalization from above. They may, however, be focused on an agenda that expresses fairly narrow specific interests. For example, a "not in my backyard"–style environmental group may be concerned only with protecting a specific geographical area from pollution by a global corporation; or a labor union may be primarily concerned with protecting the jobs of a particular group of workers against cheap imports. While they may fight militantly around "their issue," they are also willing to consider making deals at the expense of the movement as a whole if their concerns can be addressed by those in power. They lack an identification with the movement's overall vision and a commitment to all its elements.

There may also be significant differences in style and organization. Many such groups had their origins in social movements, but in many cases they have become institutionalized and bureaucratized.

In some cases, such organizations can become enemies of more activist movements. For example, for much of the 1960s and 1970s, the AFL-CIO was an active opponent of the more militant civil rights, environmental, peace, and anti-imperialist movements.

Over time, however, movements can have a major impact on such institutions. Much of the change that has taken place in organized labor in the United States during the 1990s was a result of those influenced by and participating in such militant movements developing strength within unions. Even if allies cannot be brought to full participation in the movement, weaning them away from their control by capital and the nation state is itself crucial for movement success.

The AFL-CIO's process of change regarding globalization is an interesting case in point.[1] Until the 1970s, the AFL-CIO was a strong supporter of free trade and US corporate expansion abroad. In the 1970s and 1980s, it swung over into a rather traditional economic nationalism, urging the protection of US markets through tariffs and similar barriers and showing little concern for issues beyond the protection of unionized workers' jobs. The new leadership elected in the mid-1990s gradually shifted its emphasis to global protections for labor in the global economy. And it has gradually been assimilating the need to include the interests of potential allies—for example, workers in the third world and those concerned about the environment—in its program.[2]

This process of change has been driven primarily by the failure of the previous strategies under the emerging conditions of globalization. However, it has been fostered by supporters of globalization from below in various locations inside and outside organized labor, including the globalization from below networks that run through all levels of the labor movement itself.

While the formal positions of the organized labor movement have evolved a long way toward globalization from below, its actual behavior remains highly uneven. For example, the AFL-CIO lobbied for expanded US funding for the IMF in 1998 but unexpectedly endorsed the April 16, 2000, legal demonstrations against the IMF and World Bank. It simultaneously campaigned against the admission of China into the WTO and for Al Gore, who supported it.

In such cases, an appropriate movement strategy may often be one of tension without polarization. This involves:

• Supporting those within an organization who identify with the movement, participate in its networks, and attempt to move their organizations toward it.

• Framing issues in such a way that their salience to a potential ally is clear.

• Recognizing the legitimacy of their concerns and providing them with support, like the environmentalists who started using union-label printers and the trade unionists who started using recycled paper.

• Pointing out the problems with "go it alone" strategies and laying out an easy path toward fuller participation in the broader movement for globalization from below.

The Public

The movement must keep in mind those who are at present neither its adherents nor its opponents. It is from them that passive and active supporters must be recruited. They are potential supporters of the movement's opponents. They are also capable of acting independently of either, but in ways that have a significant impact on political outcomes.

The movement interacts with public opinion on three levels: broad perspectives, specific issues, and image.

A poll taken in late 1999 by the Program on International Policy Attitudes at the University of Maryland confirms what simply talking with ordinary people suggests regarding Americans' broad perspective on globalization.[3] Most Americans define globalization as "a growing interconnectedness of the world" and regard it as somewhat more positive than negative. Of those polled, 61 percent thought the US government should "actively promote" globalization or "allow it to continue." Only 9 percent favored trying to "stop or reverse it."

But most Americans want globalization to go in a very different direction:

• 54 percent said US trade policy makers consider the concerns of multinational corporations "too much."

• 72 percent said they were giving too little consideration to working Americans.

• 60 percent said they were giving too little attention to its impact on the environment.

• 65 percent agreed that "[w]hen the World Trade Organization makes decisions, it tends to think about what's best for business, but not about what's best for the world as a whole."

• A majority thought the growth of international trade has increased the gap between rich and poor in the United States.

• An overwhelming 88 percent agreed that

[i]ncreasing international trade is an important goal for the United States, but it should be balanced with other goals, such as protecting workers, the environment, and human rights—even if this may mean slowing the growth of trade and the economy.

• 93 percent agreed that "countries that are part of international trade agreements should be required to maintain minimum standards for working conditions."

• 77 percent felt there should be more international agreements on environmental standards.

These attitudes are part of a broader philosophy: 73 percent said, "I regard myself as a citizen of the world as well as a citizen of the United States." Respondents expressed nearly the same level of concern for suffering inside and outside the United States: 74 percent agreed that "if people in other countries are making products that we use, this creates a moral obligation for us to make efforts to ensure that they do not have to work in harsh or unsafe conditions." Seventy-six percent said they would be willing to pay $25 instead of $20 for a piece of clothing that is certified as not having been made in a sweatshop. Eighty-six percent thought US companies should abide by US health and safety standards when operating outside the United States, and 88 percent said they should abide by US environmental standards. Sixty-three percent agreed that wealthier countries should allow in more of the products from very poor countries, even if this threatened the jobs of some American workers.

Seventy-eight percent agreed that "[b]ecause the world is so interconnected today, the United States should participate in efforts to maintain peace, protect human rights, and promote economic development." Two-thirds believed it was worthwhile for international organizations to intervene to correct instability in the global economy, rather than let the economy naturally adjust itself.

These views are strikingly parallel to those advocated by the partisans of globalization from below and strikingly different from both laissez-faire neoliberalism and from rightwing economic (and political) nationalism. A prime movement objective should be to reinforce and further inform this opinion. The movement should also portray itself as the champion of these views. These findings indicate, conversely, that the movement isolates itself from the public when it advocates national isolation or forms of national sovereignty that conflict with good global citizenship.

Public attitudes also have a strong class dimension. According to the Pew Research Center, only 37 percent of American families earning less than $50,000 a year hold a positive view of global free trade. The figure rises to 63 percent for families earning above $75,000, and is even more positive in higher brackets.[4]

Beyond these general perspectives, the movement engages the public primarily around specific issues, such as trade with China, ge-

netically engineered food, and child labor. Here several considerations should be kept in mind:

• Appeal must be made to feelings and concerns that the
public already accepts.

• However, the occasion must be used for broad education
and the presentation of a wider worldview.

• The issue should be presented not just as an isolated outrage, but in terms of broader global norms of which the specific issue is an expression.

• The danger of seeking to win a particular issue by framing
it in ways that undermine the unity of the movement and its allies
must be avoided. For example, it is one thing to oppose the admission of China to the WTO on the grounds that it will increase the race
to the bottom in ways that are harmful to Chinese and other third
world workers, as well as those in the United States; it is something
else to argue that it will lead to Chinese workers "stealing American
jobs."

The public is affected not only by the content of movement positions and arguments, but also by the image of the movement it ac-
quires. One of the most powerful aspects of social movements is the
attractiveness of a group of people who form a mutually supportive
community struggling for shared goals and the common good. Con-
serving and projecting this constructive character of the movement
is a crucial resource.

Most people are skeptical about the effectiveness of efforts at
social change. The activist character of the movement and its ap-
pearance as more than an ineffectual "talking shop" is also an important means of attracting support. Many people are also
frightened, however, by threats of social disruption and social up-
heaval. For many, the media presentations of confrontation in Seattle, for example, were construed not as nonviolent demonstrators
being attacked by heavily armed police, but rather as protestors
threatening public order and safety. But in those cases where the authorities' responsibility for social disruption was made clear—for
example, the police attacks on community residents that occurred in
the Capitol Hill district—public opinion placed responsibility for

disruption on the authorities and the police. Such political jujitsu is one of the key strengths of nonviolent direct action and one that the movement should cultivate.

None of this implies that the movement should not take justified but unpopular positions that conflict with the current state of public opinion or should never act in ways that some find threatening. Far from it. However, when it does so, the movement should:

• Aim to be perceived as a movement whose motivation is to serve the broad public interest, whatever disagreements there may be on the present issue.

• Frame issues in ways that present it as the representative of broad global norms against special interests. The movement should aim to be perceived as fighting for the well-being of all, rather than as selfish, self-aggrandizing, or irresponsible.

• Aim to have its goals and a wide range of its positions supported by a broad public, even if it takes a few unpopular positions along the way.

• Frame issues in ways designed to win over public opinion over time. Long-term perspective allows positioning so that accumulating catastrophes drive people into one's (well-positioned) arms.

The Right

One of the effects of globalization has been to generate a deep division within the political right. Belief in individual economic freedom and hostility to state intervention in the economy lend support to free-market globalization. But identification with the pugnacious application of national power argues for an economic nationalism that uses the power of the state to advance national interest against other nations. This division offers both opportunities and dangers for the advocates of globalization from below.

The movement for globalization from below stands opposed to both global laissez-faire and economic nationalism. It provides an alternative based on global cooperation. However, on many occasions it hears words coming from the anti-globalization right that sound almost like its own. In the United States, Pat Buchanan puts a subtly nationalistic spin on the race to the bottom:

Global-trade deals add hundreds of millions of Asians and Latin Americans to the labor pool of the industrial democracies. These new entrants into the "global hiring hall" have one thing in common: all are willing to work for a fraction of the wage than an American needs to feed, clothe, house, and educate his or her family. The global hiring hall is the greatest buyer's market in history for human labor. It puts American wage earners into direct competition for production jobs with hundreds of millions of workers all over the world.[5]

Just as Hitler appropriated the term "socialism" and its appeal for his "National Socialism," so all over the world today's right tries to appropriate an anti-globalist, anti-corporate rhetoric for its chauvinist anti-egalitarianism.

Advocates of globalization from below have often found themselves in de facto alliance with the anti-globalization right on issues such as NAFTA, WTO, and IMF, lobbying for the same votes and sometimes using the same rhetoric. Some argue that this reflects deeper common interests or values. For example, it is sometimes said that the issues are no longer between left and right, but between top and bottom, with the pro-globalization forces representing those at the top and the anti-globalization forces, whether from left or right, representing those at the bottom.[6]

Several considerations need to be kept in mind:

• The anti-globalization right, notably Pat Buchanan, still represents virulent opposition to the effort by women, minorities, gays, lesbians, and other oppressed groups to attain full respect and equality. It represents an effort to suppress cultural diversity by imposing uniform "Christian" and/or "family" values. To ally with such a force is to undermine the struggle for freedom of those it primarily aims to suppress, many of whom are central to the movement for globalization from below.

• Despite occasional anti-corporate rhetoric, the right remains hostile to popular power exercised in the interest of egalitarianism. It overwhelmingly opposes governmental protections for labor, consumers, and the environment.

• The right remains unconcerned about if not hostile to the

desire of people in the third world to receive fair treatment in the global economy. While the US right was fighting against expanded funding for the IMF, for example, it was at the same time fighting for even tighter restrictions on the social welfare activities of third world governments.

• The right defines sovereignty in a way that is hostile to the need for world law and restraint on national power. Its approach leads to the danger of a global war of all against all.

An opportunist demagogue may be more than willing to utilize the themes and rhetoric of populism to win a following. (It is reported that Pat Buchanan attentively observed Ralph Nader's speeches in the 1996 New Hampshire primary and incorporated those aspects that he found appealing.) But, as the rise of National Socialism showed, it is wise to be cautious regarding those who combine seemingly progressive and populist rhetoric with themes of national and racial chauvinism. Rather than looking to the anti-globalization right as an ally, advocates of globalization from below should regard it primarily as a competitor contending for the hearts and minds of those who are adversely affected by globalization from above.

The Electoral Arena

A striking phenomenon of the era of globalization has been the consistent assimilation of opposition parties into the neoliberal consensus once they are in power. This has happened alike with social democratic, Green, liberal, and populist parties around the world, including those such as the German Greens that started out with a conscious critique of the cooptation process.

This reflects the fact that the primary source of power in the political process is not the electorate that is supposedly represented, but economic and bureaucratic elites that dominate the real world of politics.

If the movement is to remain an independent global opposition, it needs to have its base primarily outside the electoral arena, rather than seeing its future as evolving toward a political party. This also can protect the movement from the often-justified cynicism of public opinion regarding conventional participation in the political process.

This by no means implies that the movement should simply ignore more conventional politics. It should relate to conventional politics in several ways. The movement should:

• Support genuine efforts at democratization, such as campaign finance reform.

• Treat sympathetic political figures and parties as allies, while retaining its independence.[7]

• Make demands on politicians and parties and negotiate with them.

Regional Resistance

Periodically, some kind of international regionalism is promoted as a means to escape domination of the global economy by the US Treasury Department and the US-based corporations and investors it largely represents. For example, during the Asian economic crisis of the late 1990s, Japan proposed to develop an Asian recovery agency that would provide an alternative to the US-dominated IMF rescue effort. (This proposal was quickly condemned and rejected by the US Treasury Department.)[8] US-European conflict in the WTO and the IMF has led to calls for greater European resistance to US domination. Michael Steiner, chief diplomatic adviser to German Chancellor Gerhard Schröder, complained, "We have discovered that the superpower sees its global role not only in the military arena but also in setting the rules of globalization through the IMF."[9] The global South has long asserted its specific interests as a region, most recently at the 2000 Havana meeting of the G-77, which called for its members to "promote their common interests by shaping and directing multilateral trade negotiations to take into account the needs of developing countries."[10]

Such region-based initiatives could lead in two very different directions. They could lead to destructive conflict between regions.[11] But they could also provide a force that, allied to the movement for globalization from below, might help impose a major restructuring of the global economy, especially if different regions cooperated to create an alternative to the present Washington consensus. Such initiatives would also be in accord with evolution toward a multilevel system of regulation and governance.

Frieder Otto Wolf has suggested what this approach might mean for Europe. The EU should not proclaim "I want to be Caliph instead of the Caliph!" Rather, it should proclaim:

> Let's have rule of law, instead of autocracy.... This is something that will really damage the hegemony of the US: because it can generate an alternative political consensus around the EU which the US would have great difficulty to evade in the long run. A strategy of trying to conquer the present position of the US for the EU on the contrary could expect to generate generalized mistrust and resistance.
>
> Within the WTO this should take the form of pushing back unfair rules (e.g. on the private appropriation of the "global commons" by vitiated rules of "intellectual property"...) and fighting rules of the type "the umpire defines the game" as e.g. the unabashed US dominance in the application of fair competition rules. For the areas of the "International Financial Architecture" and of global banking supervision it would mean asking for the reintroduction of binding rules going beyond precautionary self-control by the major agents themselves.... The single currency should be strategically exploited, not to compete with the US for who will be the dominant world currency, but rather offering an anchor of monetary co-operation and stabilisation to whoever really needs it, while at the same time impeding the US economic policy to interfere with the internal and endogenous development of the Euro region.... It is not a sound common European interest to try to substitute the Wall-Street complex by a London or Frankfurt complex: The EU and its member states should rather be protagonists for a realistic re-regulation of the global financial markets with the aim of cautiously "de-fusing" the present speculative "bubble," before there is an uncontrollable explosion.[12]

Such efforts have met strong US opposition. Regional resistance is most likely to succeed if it becomes inter-regional resistance and is linked to the great majority of people within the US who share its interests. While states will be a necessary part of this resistance, the basis for it needs to be established by movements in civil society.

Reform from Above

For a variety of reasons, sectors of elites periodically deviate from the straight and narrow path of neoliberalism. They may represent the interests of particular sectors of capital—for example, ones that produce nationally rather than globally or that seek government efforts to open foreign markets. They may be concerned about systemic economic crises and seek reforms to counter them. They may be concerned about the threat of social unrest. They may have personal political ambitions or be engaged in factional conflict within or among elites for which they seek allies. They may be genuinely concerned about poverty, the environment, or injustice out of ethical motives not rooted in individual or elite self-interest. Or they may be responding to pressure from the movement and its allies.

The era of globalization has seen a number of such initiatives. Examples include the reform efforts at the World Bank; the flurry of initiatives for a "new financial architecture" that followed the Asian financial crisis of the late 1990s; Clinton's embrace of labor and environmental protections in WTO agreements; and the proposals to open up the WTO to greater transparency and accountability that followed its Seattle fiasco. No doubt the future will hold many more.

Such elite reform projects offer both opportunities and dangers to the movement for globalization from below. On the one hand, they represent a split in an elite common front (for example, the breaking up of the so-called Washington consensus by these various defections). They open up public debate. They may also create a situation in which a segment of the elite needs public support to achieve its own objectives. This makes it possible to establish a bargaining process in which demands can be made and pressure brought to bear.

On the other hand, they represent a danger of cooptation of movement forces and allies and even of inadvertently strengthening enemies and establishing institutions that will be used for future oppression. The HIPC Initiative of the IMF and World Bank, for example, purported to address the need of poor countries for debt reduction, but actually demanded intensified structural adjustment conditions as the price of such debt reduction.[13]

Faced with elite reform proposals, advocates of globalization from below should evaluate those proposals' goals, making clear, when necessary, the extent to which they are intended to preserve elite domination and the flow of corporate profits. They need to present counter-proposals, drawn from the movement's own program. Then they need to define conditions for support. For example, when sectors of the elite proposed a "new architecture" for the global financial system, the movement could have agreed to support it—but only if it included cancellation of the third world debt, an end to structural adjustment conditions in international loans, and a Tobin Tax on speculative financial transactions, with the proceeds to be applied to environmentally constructive development in the third world.

The Movement Beyond the Movement

The social composition of the movement for globalization from below is rapidly changing. The NGOs that spearheaded transnational response to global issues in the 1980s and 1990s often did so from a rather narrow social base. They represented not so much globalization from below as globalization from the middle: middle class and even elite groups in the North trying to act on behalf of the global poor and humanity as a whole.[14] Initially, most US participants in the movement for globalization from below were drawn from the "new social movements" of the 1970s and 1980s, such as the environmental, human rights, peace, and anti-nuclear movements. Participants in these movements were overwhelmingly drawn from the middle class. Indeed, one of the characteristics of progressive social movements in late-20th-century America was the absence of large numbers of working class participants.[15]

The emerging movement that became so visible at the Battle of Seattle is far broader and more diverse. Globalization affects working class as well as middle class people, albeit in distinct ways, creating the possibility for a multiclass movement that can serve as a vehicle for people "across the class divide."[16] Nonetheless, it is far from incorporating or leading all of the movements for social change locally or globally. Still less does it embody the billions of people who are affected by globalization and are responding to it in ways (from fundamentalist religion to immigration) that do not fit the pattern of social movements discussed in this book.[17]

Those who currently form the movement for globalization from below could easily become closed off to these emerging forces or mistakenly try to establish hegemony over them. To avoid these pitfalls, they need to recognize that a wide range of social groups is being affected in a variety of ways by globalization from above. Such groups will inevitably develop their own responses and follow their own itineraries. They are unlikely to be subsumed under the movement in its current form.

For example, considerable concern has been expressed in the United States about the relatively modest participation by African Americans in the demonstrations in Seattle and Washington, DC.[18] The first thing to recognize is that African Americans have their own traditions of internationalism stretching back a century and a half to the struggle against slavery and through to the anti-apartheid movement. The second is that African Americans have their own reasons to be concerned about the impact of globalization from above. As National Urban League President Hugh Price put it, "The manufacturing jobs that once enabled blue collar workers to purchase their own homes and occasional new cars have all but vanished from the inner city"; and, while racism is still widespread, "the global realignment of work and wealth is, if anything, the bigger culprit."[19]

The black community in the US has in fact been making its own response to globalization. For example, African Americans played a leading role in opposing the so-called NAFTA for Africa trade bill and in supporting Representative Jesse Jackson, Jr.'s "Hope for Africa" legislation. It has also played a major role in the Jubilee 2000 campaign for debt relief. It would be patronizing to assume that the African American community should simply show up at events like the Battle of Seattle and participate on terms set by other groups.

Around the world, mass worker movements have contested globalization from above through resistance to privatization, social service cuts, and structural adjustment. May and June 2000 saw six general strikes against the effects of globalization and neoliberalism. In India, 20 million workers and farmers paralyzed much of the country with a general strike "aimed against the surrender of the country's economic sovereignty before the World Trade Organization and the International Monetary Fund," according to one leader. As many as 12 million Argentine workers struck against austerity measures the government imposed as conditions for an IMF standby loan. In Nigeria, a general strike protesting IMF-promoted fuel price increases closed much of the country. In South Korea, a partial general strike demanded a shorter workweek and labor law coverage for contingent workers to counter the impact of IMF restructuring plans. In South Africa, 4 million workers struck to protest the loss of 500,000 jobs as a result of the government's neoliberal austerity policies. A general strike in Uruguay protested high unemployment rates that workers blamed on IMF-inspired spending cuts.[20]

Recognizing these as independent forms of resistance to globalization from above does not mean that advocates of globalization from below should stand aloof from such activities. Those active in the current movement should:

• Pursue ongoing dialogue and common ground with groups affected by globalization from above that are not yet part of the movement for globalization from below.

• Include the concerns and demands of poor and oppressed groups as central concerns of the movement and central aspects of the movement's program.

• Recognize that social movements, like the societies from which they grow, are marked by the prevailing inequalities based on race, class, gender, nationality, ethnicity, and other social divides. This requires appropriate forms of compensation, such as directing resources toward groups that need greater resources in order to participate and affirmative action regarding the role of such groups in movement leadership.

• Encourage independent development of responses to globalization by impoverished and oppressed groups, without presuming that they should be subsumed under the organizational forms of the present movement.

• Provide materials and solidarity without seeking hegemony.

• Keep the movement open to new input and further evolution as new groups begin to relate to it.

• Identify and seek to correct the cultural barriers to equal participation in the movement.

• Accept as legitimate the process by which poor and oppressed groups themselves pursue a strategy of tensions by making demands on other movements for incorporation of their concerns.

Those who have been forced into contingent work provide an example of a group that is deeply affected by globalization but has not generally identified with the movement for globalization from below. An initiative by a coalition in Massachusetts illustrates how the interests of such groups can be connected to concerns about globalization. The flyer for a recent march for "Temp Worker Justice" explained, "Temp work is the face of globalization. But workers all over the world are fighting back for economic security." It tied demands for city policies, state legislation, and corporate responsibility to globalization. "The temp industry is dominated by global giants.... This march will visit a few large agencies to demand that they sign the Temp Worker Bill of Rights." The flyer was headlined, "Join a Global Fight for Justice."[21]

•

The movement for globalization from below functions, in effect, as the tip of a spear, opening up issues and positions that represent broad but denied social interests. It will be most successful if it is able to divide its opposition and bring along with it a wide range of allies.

Chapter 9

Fix It or Nix It

Strategy

Globalization from below seems puny compared to globalization from above. Loose networks of unarmed activists appear no match for those who control the world's major military machines, most of its wealth, its most powerful corporations, and its dominant governments. Yet the movement for globalization from below has won some impressive victories in its short life, from the defeat of the MAI to the passage of the protocol on genetically engineered organisms. How have those victories been achieved and how can they be extended?

As we saw in Chapter 2, the underlying vulnerability of the powerful lies in their dependence on the support or acquiescence of others. Social movement power is based on withdrawing that consent or threatening to do so. But it is a long way from that potential power to concrete actions that force change. That requires strategy.

Strategy is the means for achieving long-range goals in concrete situations. A concept with military origins, strategy literally means the choice of ground on which to engage the enemy. But the analogy to war should not be taken too literally. A social movement is different from war, or at least modern total war, in that its goal is not so much annihilating an enemy as changing social power relationships. Its terrain is not physical geography but a structured set of social relationships. The globalization from above that the movement contests is not an army or a country but a complex set of social processes and actors.

The principal strategy of the movement for globalization from below has been to identify the violation of generally held norms, demand that power actors conform to those norms, and threaten the bases of consent on which they depend if they fail to do so. This strategy is summed up in the popular movement slogan "fix it or nix it"—shorthand for "fix it or else we'll nix it."

Neither globalization from above nor globalization from below represents a unified entity. Rather, they are collections of diverse actors and forces with a variety of ends and means. The movement's ability to prevail in a conflict depends primarily on drawing together sufficient forces to impose negative consequences on opponents and on dividing and undermining opponents' support. These are essentially the means that have been used in successful movement struggles to block the MAI, cut third world debt, forestall the millennial round of the WTO, and pass the protocol on GEOs.

If the movement's crucial source of power is its ability to unify a wide range of potential supporters, its campaigns face a built-in contradiction. No one campaign can represent all the interests and accomplish all the goals of the movement as a whole. No one such struggle is going to solve all the problems of the global economy or bring all social actors into conformity with all social norms. So campaigns need to be seen in the context of a protracted struggle of which each campaign is only part of an unfolding process that involves a far longer time and a far wider social space.

Wise strategy requires a vision of the movement as a whole that transcends particular organizations and sectors. Only with such a common vision is it possible to pursue a multifaceted, coordinated, and mutually supportive strategy. As in war, a fertile source of bad strategy lies in taking short-term tactical necessities and raising them to the level of strategy.

A campaign that wins its concrete objectives but leaves the movement weak and divided can claim only a Pyrrhic victory. Conversely, even a defeated campaign can "win by losing" if it brings new participants to the movement, unifies different groups, increases the capacity for action, clarifies common interests and objectives, educates the public, or splits and weakens the opposition.

Movement strategy also involves the coordination of different elements and different styles of action. Ideally, these can be made synergistic. In the Battle of Seattle, for example, the combination of extremely militant nonviolent direct action and large numbers of supportive but less militant demonstrators created a force far more powerful than either one would have been by itself. Here the military analogy holds: coordinated air, sea, and land forces are enormously stronger than any one of them alone, even though such coordination is routinely accompanied by interservice tensions.

Social conflict is an interaction in which one party does not control the action of the others. For that reason, a strategy is very different from either a program or a plan. While a movement's goals must develop gradually over time, its strategies need to be flexible so they can adapt to rapid change. If the other side changes its strategy (for example, by turning to violent repression or seeking to open negotiations with its opponents), a movement must be able to revise its strategy in turn or face being rapidly outflanked.

A movement always contains many weaknesses and contradictions that its opponents can exploit.[1] The easiest way for a movement to be defeated is to defeat itself.

Like war, social conflict generally takes place in a murky zone in which the actual configuration of forces and the actual results of any particular course of action are more conjecture than certainty. No one strategy can fit all situations. Monsanto is not the IMF and blocking the World Bank's funding for a dam is not the same as forcing a global corporation to bargain with its employees.[2] Each campaign involves not only a unique set of forces to be mobilized, but also a concrete analysis of the balance of forces and what they allow to be accomplished.

A "fix it or nix it" strategy always involves difficult decisions about what constitutes "fixing it." While the movement's program can and should lay out broad objectives that address fundamental global problems and the needs of all parts of the movement, the demands made by a particular campaign are far more limited and the elements agreed to in a settlement may be more limited still. Given the uncertainties of social conflict, there will always be disagreements over what demands to make, when to negotiate, and what to accept in a settlement. A process for resolving these demands is one of the key needs of a movement. And people who share the same values and objectives should not allow tactical disagreements to permanently divide them.

Violations

When a violation of widely accepted norms occurs in a political system with full democracy and accountability, the system provides institutionalized mechanisms to correct the violation. But when a global corporation exploits children in third world sweatshops, or international investors destroy the livelihoods of millions of people by withdrawing investments from their country, or burning of carbon causes global warming, there is no such mechanism in place. These problems are either caused by institutions that are not accountable to those they affect or are outside the formal responsibility of any institution.

In such instances, people may appear powerless, but in fact they are not. It is precisely in situations where there is no institutionalized accountability that the hidden power of social movements comes into play. Globalization from below activists can use that power to change corporations, markets, governments, international institutions, and the rules governing them.

When widely accepted norms are violated, it can cause concern in many quarters, including both those directly affected and other people who believe in the violated norms. A network of those concerned may form or an existing network may take up the issue.

In some cases, the network may develop its own response in civil society. In response to a need for jobs, services, and housing, for example, many local groups have initiated food coops, employee-owned home-care companies, women's health clinics, nonprofit housing agencies, and other alternative enterprises. In response to exploitative conditions imposed on coffee growers and craft producers in third world countries, various groups have organized "fair trade" enterprises that purchase from producers on more just terms and seek to create market stability for them. The microlending of the Grameen Bank and the massive international aid activities of NGOs also exemplify such constructive work.

Such voluntary initiatives could conceivably be conducted on a larger scale. For example, the Alliance for Democracy in the United States has proposed a sort of "people's treaty" called "A Common Agreement on Investment and Society" to be ratified and implemented by local communities around the world.[3]

Campaigns

Sometimes such voluntary problem solving in civil society is blocked by the distribution of power. Sometimes the violation of widely accepted norms is protected by established power. And power, as the abolitionist ex-slave Frederick Douglass put it, "concedes nothing without a demand."[4] Most movement action starts with a demand on someone: World Bank, stop funding the Narmada Dam; IMF, don't encourage child labor; G-7, cut third world debt.

Demands represent a part, though not all, of what the movement seeks. They may represent specific changes, like the ending of World Bank funding of roads into the Amazon rain forest; or they may involve new rules, such as requirements that lenders to poor countries bear part of the cost of loans that are unrepayable. In either case, these demands represent the partial implementation of norms. Good demands unify supporters; divide opponents; help neutralize counter-attacks; embody parts of widely accepted norms; and represent a good so obvious that the public would naturally tend to scorn anyone who refused to concede it.

The process of working out common demands can be crucial for movement unity and effective strategy. For example, groups from around the world formed an alliance in response to the effort of governments in the OECD to negotiate the MAI. Initially, the groups were split on whether simply to oppose any agreement outright or instead to lobby for inclusion of environmental, labor, and other protections. But they then agreed to a common strategy. They

would put forward minimum conditions for fixing the MAI proposals. If these conditions were accepted by the governments, they
would agree to support further MAI negotiations. But if their common demands were not met, they would all agree to oppose the
agreement, even if some concessions were made. Their program
was not accepted, whereupon they effectively worked together to
bring the MAI negotiations to a halt.[5]

Such demands are normally accompanied by campaigns designed to pressure someone with power to concede. Campaigns utilize the withdrawal of consent in myriad forms. What ensues is a
struggle; or, as Gandhi once put it, "[T]he matter resolves itself into
one of matching forces."[6] Social movements do not enter into such
struggles primarily on the basis of membership numbers, money in
the bank, or other fixed assets they can currently deliver, but on their
potential support and the costs they might be able to impose on
their opponents in the future.

When the Empire Strikes Back

Movement demands are rarely agreed to without a fight. So success
is not just a result of movement pressure, but also of effectively resisting counter-pressure in its many forms. These typically include at
least repression, cooptation, and divide-and-conquer tactics.

Repression

From Beijing to Seattle, repression is a common last resort of challenged power, as well as a first and middle resort. But features of
globalization itself, including instantaneous global communication
and the ideology of human rights, have made repression harder to
use as a tool. International solidarity has a crucial role to play in protecting human rights against repression. For example, pressure from
the US labor movement almost certainly saved the life of imprisoned
Indonesian labor activist Muchtar Pakpahan during the final crisis of
the Suharto dictatorship, and in 1999, US labor activists demonstrated outside Texaco's Washington, DC, office to protest the use
of the army and police against strikers at an Indonesian refinery.
Amnesty International and the Sierra Club began a joint campaign

to draw attention to the persecution of environmentalists around the world, such as Rodolfo Montiel—a campesino in the state of Guerrero, Mexico, who was arrested and tortured after resisting the clear-cutting of local forests—and activists in Chad and Cameroon who have been threatened and silenced due to their opposition to Exxon and Mobil's proposals for new oil-well and pipeline construction.[7]

Over the course of the 20th century, social movements from India to Poland and from the United States to the Philippines have developed forms of nonviolent action that have provided a kind of political jujitsu for dealing with repressive violence. Rather than either submitting to repression or responding violently, these techniques resist established authority—for example, by blocking roads, occupying buildings, or demonstrating in violation of injunctions and police orders—without doing physical harm to company guards, police, soldiers, or other human beings who attempt to restore "law and order." Such disciplined nonviolent resistance became an important part of American political practice with the civil rights struggles of the 1950s and 1960s.[8] Nonviolent civil disobedience can help neutralize repression and the fear that it is intended to instill; call public attention to the justice of demands; and make clear participants' willingness to accept personal sacrifice in the interest of broader human purposes that underlie movement action.

Cooptation

Repression can be costly, messy, and bad for one's image. It is often replaced by or combined with cooptation. In the wake of the Battle of Seattle, for example, *The Economist* recommended that the WTO take a lesson from the World Bank and "try to weaken the grand coalition that attacked it in Seattle by reaching out to mainstream and technical NGOs." It indicated that NGOs, once highly critical of the World Bank, were now "surprisingly quiet." The reason: "The Bank has made a huge effort to co-opt them."[9]

> James Wolfensohn, the Bank's boss, has made "dialogue" with NGOs a central component of the institution's work. More than 70 NGO specialists work in the Bank's field offices. More than

half of World Bank projects last year involved NGOs. Mr. Wolfensohn has built alliances with everyone, from religious groups to environmentalists. His efforts have diluted the strength of "mobilisation networks" and increased the relative power of technical NGOs (for it is mostly these that the Bank has co-opted). From environmental policy to debt relief, NGOs are at the centre of World Bank policy.[10]

When such cooptation is successful, the movement or part of it ceases to be an independent force. Leaders may be drawn in and separated from their rank and file. Or organizations, like the CONGOs, are given a privileged place at the official table, but in exchange become dependent on their benefactors.

It is important to distinguish such cooptation from a willingness to engage in dialogue and negotiation. In the former, independence is lost and action is limited to what is acceptable to the patron. In the latter, discussions take place but independence remains. The difference is indicated by the fact that some, though by no means all, of the NGOs that have been involved with the World Bank nonetheless participated in the Washington, DC, demonstrations against the bank in April 2000.

Divide-and-conquer tactics

Provoking splits in the movement is a major means to defeat or even destroy it. A notorious example is the way that lumber companies in the Pacific Northwest have for years pitted environmentalists against timber workers—and laughed all the way to the sawmill.

Another blatant example is the way that promoters of the WTO have attempted to play off first world workers against the third world. Columnists who normally express little but contempt for third world people weep that American labor is crucifying the global poor. Under the heading "Workers vs. Workers," *New York Times* columnist Paul Krugman wrote that "[l]abor has decided that it must try to help American workers by denying opportunity to even needier workers abroad—while, of course, denying that it is doing any such thing."[11] President Clinton's sudden endorsement of sanctions to enforce international labor rights, whatever its short-term political motivations, was also a wedge driven between Northern unions and the global South.

Divide-and-conquer tactics have a head start when they are used against movements such as globalization from below that bring together a wide range of diverse groups and interests. It is crucial that potentially divisive issues be addressed before campaigns are launched and while they are under way. Demands must integrate the needs of different participants and means must be established to ensure that concessions are not made by one group at the expense of others. Tactical disagreements should not be allowed to turn into schisms. And the movement's overall need for unity and the responsibility of all to nourish it must be reflected not only in policy but also in the movement's life and culture.

Negotiations

There are times when a movement simply imposes its norms. Craft unions in the 19th century, for example, often passed rules, known as "craft legislation," for how work should be conducted. Then union workers refused to work for any employer who did not accept them. When 900 NGOs from 37 countries pledged to campaign for defunding of the World Bank if its loans for the Narmada Dam went ahead, the Bank didn't negotiate; it simply withdrew the loans.[12]

There are also times when an existing power center is in such disarray that it is no longer able to interfere effectively with people doing what they choose. It is no accident that most revolutions in the 20th century have come after many years of war in which the means of rule have been depleted.

Far more typical are situations in which movements are able to threaten power holders but are unable to control their response or eliminate their freedom of action. Where parties can have a big effect on each other but neither can control nor annihilate the other, some sort of tacit or formal negotiating process is likely to emerge.

Many movements have had the experience of receiving a totally unanticipated "feeler" proposing to negotiate from an opponent with whom they have been in bitter combat for years or even for generations. It happened with anti-sweatshop activists and the apparel industry; with public health advocates and the tobacco industry; and with anti–genetic engineering campaigners and Monsanto.

The idea of negotiations with "the enemy" is always a source of discomfort. Negotiating is often condemned as a recognition of an opponent's legitimacy. But entering negotiations doesn't have to be accompanied by an acceptance of the other side's right to exercise power; it can be limited to an acknowledgment that it does, in fact, exercise power and that therefore the interest of people and the environment requires that it be engaged.

Negotiations present serious dangers of splits and sell-outs. They can be exploited for self-serving purposes both by leaders who participate in them and by those who attack them from the outside. But they can sometimes realize gains for the movement that would otherwise be impossible.

Considerations for deciding whether to enter and/or stay in negotiations include:

• Will it strengthen or weaken the movement?

• Can the movement handle the negotiating process?

• Can the movement itself reach agreement on what compromises to accept?

• Can participants agree to withdraw from negotiations if they don't achieve what they decided was acceptable?

• How much will the movement have to tone down its struggle?

• Do those with whom the movement is negotiating actually have the power to make concessions?

• Is the other side likely to offer something significant?

Special problems emerge when negotiations are conducted on behalf of networks rather than institutionalized organizations with established formal procedures. Who should be represented and how should their representatives be chosen? (In some cases, parts of a network may enter negotiations while others stand apart, but both tacitly cooperate as "good cop" and "bad cop" in putting pressure on the other side.) How does a network develop a common program and strategy? How can a network conduct continuing consultation and ultimately ratify an agreement? When these questions are not answered effectively, self-defeating splits can easily emerge.[13]

For example, unions, human rights groups, and apparel corporations engaged in lengthy negotiations under the auspices of the Apparel Industry Partnership to establish a code of conduct for labor conditions in transnational corporations and a code authority to certify goods that were produced under acceptable conditions. Initially, NGOs not included in the negotiations attacked the process. After meetings that included both the labor and human rights negotiators and their critics, an "inside/outside" or "good cop/bad cop" strategy emerged. Those on the inside remained in the negotiations, but maintained that the companies' concessions were inadequate. Those on the outside generally did not condemn those participating but insisted that the concessions made were inadequate. Both continued to put pressure on the companies in the public arena. This "good cop/bad cop" cooperation broke down, however, when the inside groups split and some left the negotiations.

There are now at least three organizations involved in promoting codes of conduct and developing monitoring for US apparel corporations. An interesting dynamic has emerged as a result: the more militant organizations, notably the student-initiated Workers Rights Consortium, are setting higher standards of acceptable corporate conduct, which in turn is putting pressure on the Apparel Industry Partnership's Fair Labor Association to demonstrate that it is not merely providing window dressing for the corporations.[14]

When Power Concedes

At some point in the course of a campaign, the balance of forces starts to shift. One side begins to consider changes that it previously treated as inconceivable.

Generally speaking, power concedes when the cost of concession is less than the cost of continued resistance.[15] Those costs are partly the product of movement pressure. A stunning example was the decision of Monsanto to withdraw from the business of selling sterile seeds. This was compounded by the decision to open a dialogue with Greenpeace and to accept a genetic engineering protocol it had resisted for years.[16]

While the movement aims to win concessions to its demands, concessions can also conceal dangers. They can come with an explicit or tacit quid pro quo that can weaken or divide the movement in the future. They can cause different parts of the movement to trash each other as sell-outs or, conversely, as irrelevant and unrealistic. Or they can leave people feeling that, having won, they can go home and relax.

In a long-term perspective, negotiations, truces, and settlements do not represent the end of struggles; rather, they represent phases and aspects of a wider struggle. Within that perspective, any particular settlement can be evaluated as part of a wider movement strategy, rather than as a moral absolute that in itself either is or is not "good enough." For example, the National Labor Committee (NLC) once ran a campaign against the Gap, demanding labor rights and independent monitoring at a particular subcontractor in Central America. After an extended pressure campaign, the Gap finally sat down with the NLC and agreed to its demands. Although the NLC then halted that particular campaign, that was far from the end of anti-sweatshop campaigns against the Gap. Indeed, the Gap became the target of another campaign, launched by Global Exchange, against the continuing denial of labor rights and living wages by its contractors around the world.[17]

In a protracted struggle, "talk, talk, fight, fight" is often the strategy of choice. Indeed, a truce on one front may clear the way for more advanced struggles on others.

Any campaign has two objectives. One is to bring its target into conformity with basic social norms. The other is to strengthen the movement relative to its opponents in the future. Ideally, each campaign leaves the movement stronger for the next phase. Every reform opens to a new reform. That requires a long-term perspective and a vision of the movement as a whole that transcends particular organizations and sectors.

The Battle After Seattle

The emerging post-Seattle global campaign around the WTO provides an example of the "fix it or nix it" strategy.[18] Canadian activists

Maude Barlow and Tony Clarke spelled out the thinking behind such a campaign:

> One strategic issue arising out of Seattle … is whether to "fix" or "nix" the WTO regime. While some want to take advantage of the moment to press for reform of the WTO to make it more accountable to civil society concerns, others maintain that the model is so thoroughly flawed that we should seize the opportunity now to dismantle and replace it.

Yet, they point out, "This need not be an 'either/or' proposition."

> The *fix-it or nix-it* slogan emerging out of Seattle could be used in such a way as to combine both in building a common strategy. Instead of simply reforming the WTO, for example, a platform of radical changes could be put forward calling for a major transformation of the WTO's mandate, rules and procedures. If, as is likely, civil society's platform for change is rejected outright, then the stage could be set for demanding that the WTO be dismantled and replaced altogether. Once rejected, a fall-back strategy could be implemented, one designed to take advantage of opportunities for monkey wrenching the current negotiations in such a way as to rollback and destabilize the operations of the WTO.

Such a strategy would need to extend its focus beyond the WTO itself.

> At the same time, measures could be taken to strengthen countervailing mechanisms, such as the ILO, UNCTAD, and UNEP. All this, of course, would have to be undertaken with a vision of fundamentally transforming institutions of global governance.[19]

An international meeting in March 2000 elaborated just such a strategy under the title "WTO—Shrink or Sink! The Turn Around Agenda."

> We believe it is essential to use this moment as an opportunity to change course and develop an alternative, humane, democratically accountable and sustainable system of commerce that benefits all. This process entails rolling back the power and authority of the WTO.[20]

The statement demanded:

- No WTO Expansion
- Protect Basic Social Rights and Needs
- Protect Basic Social Services
- Restore National Patent Protection Systems
- No Patents on Life
- Food Is a Basic Human Right
- No Investment Liberalization
- Fair Trade: Special and Differential Rights for Third World Countries
- Prioritize Agreements on Social Rights and the Environment
- Democratize Decision Making
- Dispute the [dispute settlement] System

As of August 18, 2000, 514 organizations from 66 countries had signed on to the agenda.[21]

As Lori Wallach of Public Citizen's Global Trade Watch explained,

There is a list of things the WTO must do—not talk about, like they did for five years about transparency, and nothing happened.... And if those changes aren't made at the end of those 18 months or so before the next ministerial [meeting], then, not only should the United States get out, but, in fact, all of the country-based campaigns, and there are 30 of them at least, will launch campaigns either to get their countries out or to withdraw funding.[22]

By such means do the people of the world withdraw their consent from globalization from above and impose their own norms on the global economy.

Conclusion

Globalization from above represents an epoch in human history. It involves a multifaceted transformation of production, finance, political authority, and culture. It has failed to fulfill its promise of well-being for the world's people, and instead is creating more poverty, misery, and environmental destruction than the world has ever known.

The emergence of the movement for globalization from below also defines an epoch in human history. Its purpose is to counter that devastation. That is neither the work of a day nor something that will be achieved in one revolutionary cataclysm. It is something that will be accomplished through a thousand battles on a hundred fronts. Or, to change the metaphor, it is a forest that will take the planting of a thousand trees and a generation of nurturing to grow.

The movement for globalization from below has developed in myriad nooks and crannies that are marginal to dominant institutions. It has linked up across the boundaries of nations, continents, interests, and identities. It has forged a common vision and is developing a common program. It is utilizing the hidden power of social movements—the dependence of all power centers on the consent of the people—to force institutions to comply with global norms.

There is no guarantee that such a movement can actually modify globalization enough to preserve people and environment, let alone to build a decent world order. But that is more likely to be achieved by means of a movement that is unified across the boundaries of countries, issues, and constituencies than by any other approach. Protecting and expanding such a movement provides the best chance to deal with globalization in a constructive and democratic way.

Participation in that movement can also make it possible to live in a way—and in a social environment—that is less dominated by the culture and values of global capital, even if it is still constrained by them. It allows one to live in a way that asserts human values other than greed and domination. It involves politics not just as legislation and elections but as a way that people live life together. It represents not just an alternative institutional structure but an alternative way to organize life and interact with people and the world. Globalization from below represents not just a single goal but the process of democracy.

Ultimately, the problem is not to "solve" globalization. The problem is to develop social practices that can address the evolving challenges of life on Earth. We envision globalization from below eventually melding into a more general movement for social change. But right now, globalization from above is at the forefront of what social movements—and humanity—need to address.

Glossary

Autarky: National economic self-sufficiency through exclusion of foreign trade.

Battle of Seattle: Highly publicized demonstrations and confrontations with the ministerial meeting of the World Trade Organization (WTO) in late November and early December 1999.

Bretton Woods Conference: International conference in New Hampshire in July 1944 to plan postwar economic arrangements. It established what became known as the "Bretton Woods System," composed of the "Bretton Woods institutions," the International Monetary Fund (IMF) and the International Bank for Reconstruction and Development (known as the World Bank).

Economic nationalism: The use of public policy to strengthen one national economy in competition with other national economies. It includes such policies as tariffs and other barriers to trade to protect a national economy against imports and subsidies to encourage national industries. It may also involve use of national power, including trade policy, diplomacy, and war, to force other nations to change their economic policies.

General Agreement on Tariffs and Trade (GATT): International trade organization established in 1948 to reduce tariffs and other barriers to trade in goods and services. It was superseded in 1995 by the World Trade Organization.

Genetically engineered organisms (GEOs): Also known as genetically modified organisms (GMOs), these are organisms whose characteristics have been changed by manipulation of their genes.

Group of Eight Nations (G-8): The Group of Seven "rich man's club" plus Russia, which was admitted as a sort of junior partner during the 1990s.

Group of Seven Nations (G-7): The seven richest industrial countries: Canada, France, Germany, Italy, Japan, the UK, and the US. Often known as the "rich man's club," their leaders hold periodic meetings focused largely on the global economy. With the admission of Russia in the 1990s as a sort of junior partner, it is now sometimes called the Group of Eight (G-8).

Group of Seventy-Seven Nations (G-77): Group of developing countries originally formed in 1964. It currently includes 133 members who represent about 80 percent of the world's people.

Heavily Indebted Poor Country Initiative (HIPC Initiative): Effort by the IMF and World Bank to provide some debt relief for the world's poorest countries, tied to structural adjustment–type conditions.

Hegemony: A preponderance of power.

International Labor Organization (ILO): Established under the Treaty of Versailles in 1919, the ILO became affiliated with the UN in 1946. It is governed by representatives of government, business, and labor from each member country. The organization promulgates detailed labor codes and investigates violations but does not have enforcement powers.

International Monetary Fund (IMF): International organization established in 1944 to manage international currency exchange. Until 1972 it supported fixed exchange rates among different national currencies. When the United States let the dollar float, its original function vanished. The IMF then took on management of the international debt crisis, providing loans to indebted poor countries on the condition that they accept structural adjustment programs to restructure their economies.

North American Free Trade Agreement (NAFTA): An agreement effective January 1, 1994, reducing barriers to trade and investment between Canada, Mexico, and the US, and providing protection for corporations' investments and "intellectual property."

Multilateral Agreement on Investments (MAI): A proposed treaty that would limit governments' ability to regulate foreign investment. It was initially discussed by the World Trade Organization in 1996, where it was opposed by various third world countries, then discussed by the Organization for Economic Cooperation and Development (OECD), where it was blocked as a result of a worldwide citizens' campaign. Efforts continue to incorporate its elements in the WTO or the IMF.

Organization for Economic Cooperation and Development (OECD): Group of 29 industrialized nations founded in 1961.

Permanent Normal Trade Relations (PNTR): Historically, many international trade agreements have been based on the "most favored nation" principle under which one country agrees to give another's exports the most favorable treatment it offers those of any nation. To reduce opposition to providing this status to certain countries, notably China, US political leaders replaced the term "most favored nation status" with "Permanent Normal Trade Relations."

Sovereignty: A state's independent, exclusive, and absolute authority within its territorial boundaries and over its own action and people. It is generally regarded as the constitutive principle of the modern nation state system.

Structural Adjustment Programs (SAPs): Policies imposed by the World Bank and IMF on indebted countries requiring that they radically restructure their economies in exchange for loans. These policies typically include cuts in government spending, currency devaluation, export promotion, opening markets for goods, services, and investment, reducing labor and environmental protections, cutting food and energy subsidies, and raising interest rates.

Subsidiarity: The idea, developed as a fundamental principle of the European Community, that the locus of decision making should be determined not by authority over territory (i.e., sovereignty) but by the level most appropriate for the decision to be made.

Tobin Tax: A small tax on international financial transactions designed to reduce financial speculation, as well as to provide international revenue. It was originally proposed by Nobel Prize–winning economist James Tobin.

United Nations Conference on Trade and Development (UNCTAD): An ongoing conference, first convened in 1964 on the initiative of third world countries, to address problems of underdevelopment.

World Bank: Common name for the International Bank for Reconstruction and Development, established at the Bretton Woods Conference in 1944 to aid postwar reconstruction and development. As postwar reconstruction was completed, it redefined its role as supporting development projects and structural adjustment programs in poor countries.

World Trade Organization (WTO): International organization established in 1995 to supercede the General Agreement on Tariffs and Trade (GATT). The WTO makes and enforces rules for global trade, very broadly defined, by which members are bound to abide.

Notes

Notes to Introduction

1. Steven Greenhouse, "After Seattle, Unions Point to Sustained Fight on Trade," *New York Times,* December 6, 1999, p. A28.

2. Elaine Bernard, "The Battle in Seattle: What Was That All About?" *Washington Post,* December 5, 1999, p. B1.

3. Naomi Klein, "Rebels in Search of Rules," *New York Times,* December 2, 1999.

4. Jeremy Brecher and Tim Costello, *Global Village or Global Pillage: Economic Reconstruction from the Bottom Up,* 2nd ed. (Cambridge: South End Press, 1998). For an introduction to the subject, see also Sarah Anderson, John Cavanagh, and Thea Lee, *The Field Guide to the Global Economy* (New York: New Press, 2000).

Notes to Chapter 1: Globalization and Its Specter

1. Some analysts still debate to what extent globalization is genuine or significant. See, for example, Doug Henwood, "What Is Globalization Anyway?" ZNet Commentary, November 26, 1999, maintaining that globalization is exaggerated (http://zmag.org/ZSustainers/ZDaily/1999-11/26henwood.htm), and Richard Du Boff and Edward Herman, "Questioning Henwood on Globalization," ZNet Commentary, December 1, 1999, finding Henwood's arguments "incomplete and unconvincing" (http://zmag.org/ZSustainers/ZDaily/1999-12/01herman.htm).

2. For a more detailed analysis of the first phase of globalization, see Brecher and Costello, *Global Village or Global Pillage,* and works cited there. For a review of developments up to 1998, see the Introduction to the second edition.

3. John Tagliaubue, "For Americans, an Indirect Route to the Party," *New York Times,* June 14, 1998, p. 3: 4, citing James E. Carlson, economist at Merrill Lynch in New York.

4. Anderson et al., *Field Guide to the Global Economy,* p. 12.

5. Roger Cohen, "Argentine Economy Reborn but Still Ailing," *New York Times,* February 6, 1998, p. A1.

6. John Cavanagh and Sarah Anderson, "The Impact of Capital Flows on Workers in the Global Economy," March 1, 1998, Institute for Policy Studies; "Toward a New Financial System," *The Economist,* April 11, 1998.

7. For the globalization of the process of technological change, see Peter Dorman, "Actually Existing Globalization," prepared for "Globalization and Its (Dis)Contents," Michigan State University, April 3, 1998, pp. 4–7.

8. Bennett Harrison, *Lean and Mean: The Changing Landscape of Corporate Power in the Age of Flexibility* (New York: Basic Books, 1994), pp. 9, 171. For further discussion of changing corporate and work structures and their implications for labor organization, see Jeremy Brecher and Tim Costello, "Labor and the Dis-Integrated Corporation," *New Labor Forum* 2 (Spring/Summer 1998): 5ff.

9. For a view emphasizing the similarity between contemporary globalization and previous periods of shift in global hegemony, see Giovanni Arrighi and Beverly J. Silver, *Chaos and Governance in the Modern World System* (Minneapolis: University of Minnesota Press, 1999). For a view that globalization is replacing traditional national imperialism with a universal, non-national system of empire, see Michael Hardt and Antonio Negri, *Empire* (Cambridge: Harvard UP, 2000).

10. *New York Times Magazine,* March 28, 1999.

11. Economists often discuss such failings under the heading "market failures." For further discussion of market failures and "political failures," see Jeremy Brecher, *"Can'st Thou Draw Out Leviathan with a Fishhook?"* (Washington: Grassroots Policy Project, 1995), and Charles E. Lindblom, *Politics and Markets* (New York: Basic Books, 1977), Chapters 5 and 6.

12. Clifford Krauss, "Injecting Change Into Argentina: New President Tries to Keep Industry from Leaving the Country," *New York Times,* March 8, 2000, p. C1. See also Craig Torres and Matt Moffett, "Neighbor-Bashing: Argentina Cries Foul as Choice Employers Beat a Path Next Door," *Wall Street Journal,* May 2, 2000, p. 1.

13. "Canada's Tax Cut Underwhelms Businesses: CEOs Fault Slowness of Phase-In and Look Abroad for Expansion," *Wall Street Journal,* May 2, 2000, p. A23.

14. United Nations Development Program (UNDP), *Human Development Report 1999* (New York: Oxford UP, 1999).

15. James D. Wolfensohn, "Let's Hear Everyone and Get on with Imaginative Solutions," *International Herald Tribune,* January 28, 2000 (http://www.iht.com/).

16. *World Employment Report, 1996/97* (Geneva: ILO, 1996).

17. Lawrence Mishel, Jared Bernstein, and John Schmitt, *The State of Working America 1998–99* (Ithaca: Economic Policy Institute/Cornell UP, 1999).

18. Anderson et al., *Field Guide to the Global Economy,* p. 53. *Business Week,* April 20, 1998.

19. UNDP, *Human Development Report 1999,* p. 37.

20. Fareed Zakaria, "Will Asia Turn Against the West?" *New York Times,* July 10, 1998, p. A15.

21. Reuters, "Worker Rights Key to Development," January 8, 2000.

22. Anderson et al., *Field Guide to the Global Economy,* p. 69.

23. Jan Pronk, "Globalization: A Developmental Approach," in Jan

Nederveen Pieterse ed., *Global Futures: Shaping Globalization* (London: Zed Books, 2000), p. 48.

24. "Network Guerrillas," *Financial Times*, April 30, 1998, p. 20.

25. Hilary French, *Vanishing Borders: Protecting the Planet in the Age of Globalization* (New York: Norton, 2000), p. 27.

26. Hilary French, *Vanishing Borders*, p. 8.

27. "There are strong indications that a disturbing change in disease patterns has begun and that global warming is contributing to them," according to Paul Epstein, associate director of Harvard Medical School's Center for Health and the Global Environment. Quoted in Hilary French, *Vanishing Borders*, p. 46.

28. Hilary French, *Vanishing Borders,* pp. 8–9.

29. "Das Kapital Revisited," *Financial Times*, August 31, 1998, p. 14.

30. As far as we have been able to determine, the terms "globalization from above" and "globalization from below" were coined by Richard Falk and first appeared in print in Jeremy Brecher, John Brown Childs, and Jill Cutler eds., *Global Visions: Beyond the New World Order* (Boston: South End Press, 1993). This book provides a view of the development of transnational social movements and common vision prior to 1993; it reflects an awareness of the increasing global interconnectedness in the post–Cold War era, but it puts limited emphasis on the global economic integration that was then gathering steam. For movements in the early 1990s responding specifically to economic globalization, see Chapter 5 of *Global Village or Global Pillage*. See also Richard Falk, *Predatory Globalization: A Critique* (Malden, Massachusetts: Blackwell, 1999), especially Chapter 8.

31. Jeremy Brecher, "The Opening Shot of the Second Ecological Revolution" *Chicago Tribune*, August 16, 1988.

32. "Poor Countries Draft Proposal On Poverty," *New York Times,* April 12, 2000. The G-77 currently has 133 member nations.

33. Mark Ritchie, quoted in *Global Village or Global Pillage,* p. 97.

34. According to labor journalist Kim Moody,

In the last couple of years there have been at least two dozen political general strikes in Europe, Latin America, Asia, and North America. This phenomenon began in 1994. There have been more political mass strikes in the last two or three years than at any time in the 20th century.

Kim Moody, "Workers in a Lean World," a speech to the Brecht Forum in New York, New York, November 14, 1997. Broadcast on Alternative Radio (tape and transcript available from http://www.alternativeradio.org).

35. Vandana Shiva, "The Historic Significance of Seattle," December 10, 1999, MAI-NOT Listserve, Public Citizen Global Trade Watch.

36. Howard Zinn, "A Flash of the Possible," *The Progressive* 61: 1 (January 2000). Available on-line at https://secure.progressive.org/zinn001.htm.

37. For a portrayal of current struggles as a continuation of historical working class struggles, see Boris Kargarlitsky's recent trilogy *Recasting Marxism*, including *New Realism, New Barbarism: Socialist Theory in the Era of Globalization* (London: Pluto

Press, 1999), *The Twilight of Globalization: Property, State and Capitalism* (London: Pluto Press, 1999), and *The Return of Radicalism: Reshaping the Left Institutions* (London: Pluto Press, 2000).

38. It is often pointed out that globalization is creating a capitalism that in significant ways resembles the capitalism that preceded World War I. It could also be observed that globalization from below in some ways resembles the international socialist movement before World War I. Globalization provides an opportunity to reevaluate some of the key features of the post-1914 left, such as its relationship to nationalism and the nation state; the schisms between social democracy, Communism, and anarchism; and the development of organizational forms adapted to the effort to secure state power via reform or revolution.

Notes to Chapter 2: The Power of Social Movements

1. For a fuller discussion of this subject, with extensive references, see Gene Sharp, *The Politics of Nonviolent Action: Part One: Power and Struggle* (Boston: Porter, Sargent, 1973), "Why Do Men Obey?" pp. 16–24.

2. The analysis of "hegemony" is generally associated with the work of Antonio Gramsci. See for example Antonio Gramsci, *The Modern Prince and Other Writings* (New York: International Publishers, 1959).

3. E.P. Thompson describes this process of group formation for the specific case of class: "Class happens when some men, as a result of common experiences (inherited or shared), feel and articulate the identity of their interests as between themselves, and as against other men whose interests are different from (and usually opposed to) theirs." E.P. Thompson, *The Making of the English Working Class* (New York: Vintage, 1996), p. 9.

4. Solidarity can take a number of forms. Peter Waterman defines six meanings of international solidarity:

- Identity = solidarity of common interest and identity.
- Substitution = standing in for those incapable of standing up for themselves.
- Complementarity = exchange of different needed/desired goods/qualities.
- Reciprocity = exchange over time of identical goods/qualities.
- Affinity = shared cross-border values, feelings, ideas, identities.
- Restitution = acceptance of responsibility for historical wrong.

He points out that each of these has certain problems and limitations. For example, identity-based solidarity tends to exclude those who don't share the common identity as defined; substitution can lead to an unequal, patronizing relationship of charity. See Peter Waterman, *Globalization, Social Movements, and the New Internationalisms* (London: Mansell, 1999). Preliminary text available on-line at http://www.antenna.nl/~waterman/dialogue.html.

The process of constructing solidarity is illustrated with numerous labor history examples in Jeremy Brecher, *Strike! Revised and Updated Edition* (Cambridge: South End Press Classics, 1999) and analyzed on p. 284.

5. This highly schematic formulation is based primarily on the study and observation of social movements, combined with theories drawn from many sources, for example, Jean-Paul Sartre, *Critique de la Raison Dialectique* [*Critique of Dialectical Reason*] (Paris: Gallimard, 1960), and Francesco Alberoni, *Movement and Institution* (New York: Columbia UP, 1984).

6. Bertolt Brecht, *Deutsche Kriegsfibel* ["German War Primer"], in *Gesammelte Werke* (Berlin: Suhrkamp, 1967), vol. 4, p. 638. The translation by Martin Esslin originally appeared in Jeremy Brecher and Tim Costello, *Common Sense for Hard Times* (New York: Two Continents/Institute for Policy Studies, 1976), p. 240.

7. In the "acquiescent state," people's relation to each other is mediated via the market or common relations to authority. The process of movement creation and group formation to some degree replaces these with direct relations. Sartre analyzes this as the transition from the "series" to the "group" (*Critique de la Raison Dialectique*).

8. Written by Ralph Chaplin.

9. Gene Sharp, who analyzes hundreds of historical examples of nonviolent action in the three volumes of his *Politics of Nonviolent Action* (Boston: Porter Sargent, 1973), concludes that the base of nonviolent action is "the belief that the exercise of power depends on the consent of the ruled who, by withdrawing that consent, can control and even destroy the power of their opponent" (*Part One: Power and Struggle,* p. 4). Sharp emphasizes that nonviolent struggle requires indirect strategies that undermine the opponents' strength rather than annihilate the opponent. (Of course, the picture is made less simple by the fact that "the ruled" are not a homogeneous group, and those who withdraw consent may be defeated by those who do not.) This analysis does not apply exclusively to nonviolence. Even in war, victory usually results not from physical annihilation of the enemy but from the withdrawal of support of the population from the war effort ("loss of morale"), defection of political supporters of the war, withdrawal of allies, and change in policy by ruling groups in response to the presence or threat of these factors.

10. Sharp, *Part Two: The Methods of Nonviolent Action* (Boston: Porter Sargent, 1973). See also *Part Three: The Dynamics of Nonviolent Action* (Boston: Porter Sargent, 1973).

11. In constitutional terms, this would be described as a form of nullification.

12. Of course, an irrational ruler may not be deterred from acting to repress a nonviolent movement by the fact that doing so may undermine his or her own power. But given an irrational ruler, violence is no more guaranteed to be an effective deterrent than nonviolence.

13. "United States negotiators gave in to a demand from Europe and most of the rest of the world for what is known as the 'precautionary principle'.... Even Greenpeace, an avowed critic of the technology, issued a statement calling the protocol a 'historic step towards protecting the environment and consumers from the dangers of genetic engineering.'" *St. Louis Post-Dispatch*, January 30, 2000.

The British Environment Minister, Michael Meacher, said: "For the first time countries will have the right to decide whether they want to import GM products or not when there is less than full scientific evidence. It is official that the environment rules aren't subordinate to the trade rules. It's been one hell of a battle."

"This protocol is a campaign victory in that it acknowledges that GMOs [genetically modified organisms] are not the same as other crops and products and they require that special measures be taken," said Miriam Mayet of the Malaysia-based Third World Network ... The US State Department declined to specify whether the biotechnology company Monsanto had been consulted over the past few days. A State Department source said: "We understand there is no major problem so far as the company is concerned."

The Observer, January 30, 2000.

14. As Gramsci put it, "The fact of hegemony undoubtedly presupposes that the interests and strivings of the groups over which the hegemony will be exercised are taken account of, that a certain balance of compromises be formed, that, in other words, the leading group makes some sacrifices" (*Modern Prince,* p. 154).

15. This critique has long been elaborated in the anarchist and libertarian socialist traditions, and has more recently been developed by the New Left of the 1960s, the Green movement, and the Mexican Zapatistas.

16. See Chapter 3 for an elaboration of this argument. This is not to argue that states are no longer of significance, or that political parties and contests for government power have not played an important role in the past and might not today or in the future. Rather, it is to deny that social movements can or should be reduced to such a strategy.

17. Michael Mann, *The Sources of Social Power: Volume 1* (Cambridge: Cambridge UP, 1986), Chapter 1, "Societies as Organized Power Networks."

18. Michael Mann, *Sources of Social Power,* p. 522.

19. Michael Mann, *Sources of Social Power,* p. 21.

20. We use the term *values* to refer to criteria for classifications of good and bad or of better and worse. We use the term *norms* for the application of such values to the behavior of particular classes of actors, thereby specifying how they should act.

21. Over time, the labor and socialist movements of course became increasingly focused on national governments and increasingly contained within national frameworks.

22. This threat, strongly resented by many third world governments, contributed to the deadlocking of the WTO negotiations.

23. For example, provoking such general social unrest was an articulated objective of many US opponents of the Vietnam War after other means of halting it had failed and public opinion had swung against it without visible effect on policy.

24. For a similar perspective on how social movements make change through imposing norms, with recent examples and proposals for the future, see Richard Falk, "Humane Governance for the World: Reviving the Quest," in Pieterse ed, *Global Futures,* pp. 23ff. See also *On Humane Governance: Toward a New Global Politics* (University Park, Pennsylvania: Pennsylvania State UP, 1995).

25. "Bolivian Water Plan Dropped After Protests Turn Into Melees," *New York Times,* April 11, 2000. For further information on the Cochabamba water struggle, prepared by Jim Schultz, a Cochabamba resident who played a major role in mobilizing global support for the struggle, visit http://www.americas.org.

26. *ICEM Info* 3 (1996) and *ICEM Info* 4 (1996); see also *Labor Notes,* October 1994, July 1996, and December 1996.

27. Donald G. McNeil, Jr., "As Devastating Epidemics Increase, Nations Take on Drug Companies," *New York Times,* July 9, 2000, and *Toronto Star,* May 12, 2000.

28. For information on the FAT–UE alliance, visit the UE web site at http://www.ranknfile-ue.org/international.html.

29. Two classic explorations of this dynamic are Robert Michels, *Political Parties: A Sociological Study of the Oligarchical Tendencies of Modern Democracy* (Glencoe: Free Press, 1949), and Sidney Webb and Beatrice Webb, *The History of Trade Unionism,* 2nd ed. (London: Longmans, Green, 1902). This process is analyzed by Sartre in terms of the dissolution of a group back into a series. As Alberoni points out, some degree of such re-serialization is probably inevitable, but it can be limited by practices that provide for periodical reconstitution of the group. Those hostile to social movements sometimes maintain that tyranny is their normal or only possible outcome. A classic example is Norman Cohn, *The Pursuit of the Millennium* (London: Secker and Warburg, 1957). For a discussion of these issues in the context of various left traditions, see Staughton Lynd, "The Webbs, Lenin, Rosa Luxemburg," in *Living Inside Our Hope: A Steadfast Radical's Thoughts on Rebuilding the Movement* (Ithaca: Cornell UP, 1997), pp. 206ff.

Notes to Chapter 3: Two, Three, Many Levels

1. Terry Boswell and Chris Chase-Dunn, *The Spiral of Capitalism and Socialism* (Boulder: Lynn Reiner, 1999). Boswell and Chase-Dunn do not portray the move from world polity to a world state as inevitable.

2. Patrick Bond, "Workers of the World, Transcend the Wedge!" ZNet Commentary, February 23, 2000 (http://www.zmag.org). Such concerns about the undemocratic character of global institutions are fully warranted, not because they are global, but because actually existing global institutions such as the IMF, World Bank, and WTO currently function as little more than agents of global capital.

3. Hedley Bull, *The Anarchical Society: A Study of Order in World Politics* (New York: Columbia UP, 1977), p. 245. At the time his book was written, Hedley Bull was only describing an emerging tendency. See also the discussion in Margaret E. Keck and Kathryn Sikkink, *Activists Beyond Borders: Advocacy Networks in International Politics* (Ithica: Cornell UP, 1998), pp. 209ff.

4. Within the historical range of governing institutions, those that are emerging in the transnational arena today are quite un-statelike. Globalization is indeed promoting "a world polity of global institutions" with "global governance." But this differs radically from historical nation states (no doubt the reason its description requires arcane terms like "polity" and "governance"). There are several ways in which today's emerging global institutions differ from traditional nation states.

First, organizations like the IMF, World Bank, and WTO make no claim to exclusive sovereignty over a territory to the exclusion of other entities, whether those be nations or other international institutions. Today's global institutions may interfere with nation state sovereignty, but they do not claim exclusive jurisdiction over any territory.

Second, today's global institutions are not self-legitimating. State legitimization originally ran from God to monarch to state institutions. Then the state became its own legitimization (as in the formulation of Bartolus that the Italian city-states should be recognized as "independent associations not recognizing any superior" or as in "raison d'état"). For background on the origins of state sovereignty, see Quentin Skinner, *The Foundations of Modern Political Thought* (Cambridge: Cambridge UP, 1978); Bartolus quote, p. 351. Finally, popular sovereignty legitimated the state. There is no equivalent legitimization for the IMF, World Bank, or WTO. (Perhaps there is a bit for the UN: despite its formal control by nations, it has developed a certain direct legitimization from its status as representative of the world's people.) The legitimization of the IMF, World Bank, and WTO is still derived from nation states. For historical background, see also Jeremy Brecher, "The 'National Question' Reconsidered," *New Politics*, new series, 1: 3 (Summer 1987): 95–111.

Third, historically the modern state arose as part of a system of states shaped largely by their interactions with each other. For today's global institutions, there are no such military, diplomatic, and other "external relations." (On the centrality of "external relations" in the formation of states, see Michael Mann, *Sources of Social Power*.)

Fourth, today's global institutions exhibit nothing like the monopoly of military force maintained by nation states. The ambiguous and evolving relation between militarism and globalization is an important issue beyond the scope of this book. Thomas L. Friedman argues that

> Globalization requires a stable power structure.... The hidden hand of the market will never work without a hidden fist.... And the hidden fist that keeps the world safe for Silicon Valley's technologies to flourish is called the US Army, Air Force, Navy and Marine Corps.

Thomas L. Friedman, *The Lexus and the Olive Tree: Understanding Globalization* (New York: Farrar, Straus and Giroux, 1999), p. 375. But ironically, this stunning statement is made as part of a tirade against American capitalists for not sharing this view. "For too many executives in Silicon Valley there is no geography or geopolitics anymore. When I asked an all too typical tech exec on a 1998 visit to Silicon Valley when was the last time he had talked about Iraq or Russia or foreign wars, he proudly answered: 'not more than once a year'" (p. 373). For further discussion of the relation between globalization and militarism, visit the International Network on Disarmament and Globalization web site at http://www.indg.org.

5. F.H. Hinsley, *Sovereignty* (New York: Basic Books, 1966), p. 1. For recent political science thinking on the "unpacking" of sovereignty from such an absolutist

definition, see Karen T. Litfin ed., *The Greening of Sovereignty in World Politics* (Cambridge: MIT Press, 1998). See also Brecher et al., *Global Visions*.

6. See, for example, Tim Lang and Colin Hines, *The New Protectionism: Protecting the Future Against Free Trade* (New York: New Press, 1993). This book reflects a frequent tendency among progressive advocates of withdrawal from the global economy to fluctuate among advocating national economic sovereignty, local economic self-reliance, and a multilevel approach like the one sketched below.

7. See Patrick Buchanan, *The Great Betrayal: How American Sovereignty and Social Justice Are Being Sacrificed to the Gods of the Global Economy* (Boston: Little, Brown, 1998).

8. The term "delinking" was popularized by African economist Samir Amin. See his *Delinking* (London: Zed Books, 1990). Delinking was the basic strategy of third world nationalism during the 1960s and 1970s, both in economic development strategy (e.g., "import substitution") and in "two, three, many Vietnams" resistance to imperialism. It was not a success, even at the height of third world power, and even with Chinese and Russian backing. Any advocacy of a return to such a strategy needs to deal with the reasons for these failures and the reasons to believe they won't be repeated in today's far less hospitable global economic environment.

National elites and states are overwhelmingly committed to neoliberalism and show little genuine interest in such a program. An advocate of delinking acknowledges,

> Most leaders and parties of Second and Third World societies who at one point (at least momentarily) carried the aspirations of a mass-popular electorate rapidly reversed allegiance.... Selling out the poor and working classes on behalf of international finance was also the general fate of so many labour and social democratic parties in Western Europe, Canada and Australia. Even where once-revolutionary parties remained in control of the nation-state ... ideologies wandered over to hard, raw capitalism.

Patrick Bond, "Global Economic Crisis: A View from South Africa," August 1999, available on-line at http://www.aidc.org.za/. Bond provides many examples to support this claim. There is not some national political structure which, if delinked from global capital, would start eagerly to pursue an alternative national development strategy.

When he began promoting the concept of delinking more than a decade ago, Samir Amin emphasized that "Delinking is not synonymous with autarky." See Samir Amin, "Preface," in A. Mahjoub ed., *Adjustment or Delinking: The African Experience* (London: Zed Books, 1990), pp. xii–xiii. However, a strong case can be made that delinking is tantamount to autarky—national economic isolation—under today's conditions. Imagine a single country withdrawing from the WTO, refusing to service its debt, and putting a full array of progressive requirements on foreign investment. Aside from the obvious short-term consequences (e.g., inability to acquire parts, machinery, or raw materials, except by barter), it would be cut off in the long run from modern technology, the Internet, and everything else that is developed in the global economy. This is a formula for permanent underdevelopment.

Of course, a different global economic environment would not impose these consequences, but that is exactly the point. The global economic environment must be changed to make national development possible.

9. Steven Rattner, "Europe Can't Heal Britain's Economy," *New York Times*, December 9, 1990.

10. National capital controls are sometimes urged as a solution to the problem of capital flight. While such controls may well have a constructive role to play, their effectiveness in the era of globalization is quite limited unless national policy is supported by international cooperation. It is too easy for capital to flow around such controls and too easy for investors to withdraw from countries that impose such controls unilaterally. The capital controls instituted by Malaysia at the height of the Asian financial crisis, for example, were somewhat effective in the short run but within two years they were largely dismantled by the government that had established them. The difficulty of a country unilaterally maintaining such capital controls has led Jane D'Arista and other experts to propose new international institutional mechanisms as the only way in which capital controls and other nation-state interventions can be made viable. See Jane D'Arista, "Financial Regulations in a Liberalized Global Economy," paper prepared for the Conference on International Capital Markets and the Future of Economic Policy, Queens' College, University of Cambridge, April 16–17, 1998. For related work, visit the web site of the Financial Markets Center at http://www.fmcenter.org.

11. More generally, both internal and external pressure are needed to control "rogue nations." Those of us who have spent a good part of our lives struggling against US imperialism feel a particular concern not to legitimate claims of national sovereignty that have been repeatedly used to justify US violations of international law.

12. Patrick Bond, "A View from South Africa."

13. David Harvey, "The Geography of Class Power," in Leo Panitch and Colin Leys eds., *The* Communist Manifesto *Now: Socialist Register 1998* (New York: Monthly Review Press, 1998), p. 72. For elaboration of his views, see David Harvey, *Spaces of Hope* (Berkeley: University of California Press, 2000).

14. The UN structure represents states, not people. The great powers dominate the Security Council. The General Assembly's one-state–one-vote structure provides grossly unequal representation for the world's people. Nonetheless, the UN is the only global institution that is widely recognized as providing legitimate limits on the actions of nation states. Poor countries hold a large majority in the General Assembly. The UN is rare among institutions in maintaining a mode of discourse based on common global interests.

15. Advocates of such a system can be divided into those who see it as emerging from the present power configuration represented by the G-7, World Bank, IMF, WTO, and the US Treasury Department and those who see it emerging as an alternative and an opponent to these forces.

16. See, for example, Michael H. Shuman, *Going Local: Creating Self-Reliant Communities in a Global Age* (New York: Free Press, 1998). The conflict between localist and nationalist alternatives to globalization is put in sharp relief by the controversy over the World Bank's new inspection panel, to which people directly affected by World Bank programs can appeal over the heads of their own governments. The World Bank board recently overruled the Bank's leadership to block a resettlement plan in Qinghai Province that would have affected Tibetans who had traditionally used the area. The decision, based on an unfavorable inspection panel report, was supported by the United States and other first world countries and opposed by China and most developing nations. See Joseph Kahn, "World Bank Rejects China's Proposal to Resettle Farmers," *New York Times,* July 8, 2000. For background on the World Bank inspection panel issue, see Jai Sen, "A World to Win—But Whose World Is it, Anyway?" in John W. Foster and Anita Anand eds., *Whose World Is It Anyway?: Civil Society, the United Nations, and the Multilateral Future* (Ottawa: United Nations Association in Canada, 1999), pp. 337–90.

17. See Ryan Lizza, "The Man Behind the Anti–Free-Trade Revolt: Silent Partner," *New Republic,* January 10, 2000.

18. Such a multilevel approach allows a much more differentiated analysis of the strategic field. For example, it is widely agreed in the movement that structural adjustment should be abolished. But is that equivalent to abolition of the IMF and World Bank? Or do they have some legitimate functions? For example, the original Keynesian function of the IMF in ensuring that short-term currency imbalances don't lead to competitive devaluations is at least as necessary today as in John Maynard Keynes's day, if only to make "national Keynesianism" possible. That function actually needs to be expanded, but also put under the control of a more democratic overseer, for example the UN. Similarly, some mechanism is needed to regulate aggregate demand globally, along the lines of former German finance minister Oskar Lafontaine's proposals for coordinated growth policies, initially ad hoc, eventually to be institutionalized. Their time clearly had not come, but had a deeper crisis put them on the agenda, the movement for globalization from below might well find them worthy of critical support. Total abolition of the World Bank is widely rejected even by many militant critics of structural adjustment on the grounds that the poorest countries survive only through World Bank support.

19. Ultimately, the ability of people to organize themselves to control political institutions is the only guarantee of democratic accountability, whether at local, national, or global levels.

20. Walden Bello, "Reforming the WTO Is the Wrong Agenda," in Kevin Danaher and Roger Burbach eds., *Globalize This!: The Battle Against the World Trade Organization and Corporate Rule* (Monroe, Maine: Common Courage Press, 2000), p. 117.

21. These functions are discussed in much greater detail in Chapter 6, "Draft of a Global Program." Most of these functions can be performed, to a degree, at different levels and by either state or civil society. For example, both unions and government wage regulation take labor out of competition. Governmental or nongovernment banks can supply capital to poor areas. Economic development programs can be public (like the Greater London Council's classic Greater London

Enterprise Board) or private (like the Mondragon cooperatives in the Basque region of Spain).

22. Elise Boulding, "Ethnicity and New Constitutive Orders," in Brecher et al., *Global Visions*, p. 219.

23. Joseph Henri Jupille, "Sovereignty, Environment, and Subsidiarity in the European Union," in Litfin, *Greening of Sovereignty in World Politics,* p. 243. Note that the subsidiarity principle can also be used as a basis for higher-level institutions to abandon their responsibilities and set lower-level jurisdictions up for failure. Part of the "local empowerment agenda" of US conservatives consists of giving greater responsibility to municipalities without providing the financial resources needed to fulfill those responsibilities. The "subsidiarity principle" has been invoked by the South African government in declining to intervene in the desperate problems of townships overburdened by the legacy of apartheid.

24. Jupille, p. 242. Subsidiarity differs from classic federalism in that functions rather than authority are distributed among the different levels of the system. Many modern federalist systems, including the US government, have in practice evolved toward subsidiarity.

25. Jupille, p. 243.

26. For more concrete elaboration and examples of what this means in practice, see Chapter 6 below.

27. "WTO—Shrink or Sink!" is available in the WTO section of the Public Citizen web page at http://www.tradewatch.org.

28. This is seen, for example, in the growing use of courts to challenge corporate actions in other countries and in the World Bank's new inspection panel. As political scientist Hedley Bull predicted in 1977,

> Carried to its logical extreme, the doctrine of human rights and duties under international law is subversive of the whole principle that mankind should be organized as a society of sovereign states. For, if the rights of each man can be asserted on the world political stage over and against the claims of his state, and his duties proclaimed irrespective of his position as a servant or a citizen of that state, then the position of the state as a body sovereign over its citizens, and entitled to command their obedience, has been subject to challenge, and the structure of the society of sovereign states has been placed in jeopardy. The way is left open for the subversion of the society of sovereign states on behalf of the alternative organizing principle of a cosmopolitan community.

The Anarchical Society, p. 146.

29. Muto Ichiyo, "For an Alliance of Hope," in Brecher et al., *Global Visions*, p. 156. Muto's approach severs the longstanding connection between peoplehood, territory, and sovereignty. Traditional doctrines of popular sovereignty have long been fraught with difficulty regarding who should be regarded as "a people" and how the territory of the earth should be assigned to such groups. The doctrine originally emerged in the English Revolution not to empower the people but rather to justify the authority of a Parliament that represented the landed gentry. For the origins and some of the contradictions within the doctrine of popular sovereignty, see Edmund S. Morgan, *Inventing the People: The Rise of Popular Sovereignty in England and America* (New York: Norton, 1988).

30. Kofi Annan, "The Legitimacy to Intervene," *Financial Times,* January 10, 2000, p. 19.

31. This represents an extension of the basic democratic doctrine that "governments derive their just powers from the consent of the governed."

32. "UNCTAD X: Pies, preachers and poets," *Focus on Trade* 46 (February 2000). Available on-line at http://focusweb.org.

33. "UNCTAD X." The search for legitimacy for international institutions leads to a haunting echo of the doctrine of the divine right of kings. Camdessus once described his work at the IMF as "part of the building of the Kingdom of God," and World Bank President James Wolfensohn recently stated that we can "complete the work of God" ("UNCTAD X").

Notes to Chapter 4: Handling Contradictions

1. For background on the Narmada campaigns, see Jai Sen, "A World to Win," and the International Rivers Network web site at http://www.irn.org/. For background on Bridgestone/Firestone, see Kate Bronfenbrenner and Tom Juravich, "Strategic Contract Campaigns in the Global Economy: The Steelworkers' Campaign at Bridgestone/Firestone," paper presented at 2000 AFL-CIO/UCLEA Education Conference, April 13–15, 2000, Milwaukee, Wisconsin.

2. *Americans on Globalization: A Study of US Public Attitudes, Summary of Findings* (University of Maryland: Program on International Policy Attitudes, November 16, 1999).

3. For the text of the Alternatives for the Americas Program, go to http://www.web.net/comfront/alts4americas/intro.html; for the text of *The People's Plan for the 21st Century,* go to http://www.hr-alliance.org/pp21; for the text of the NGO statement from the 2000 UNCTAD meetings, go to http://focusweb.org/unctad/unc_con.htm; for the text of "WTO—Shrink or Sink!" go to http://www.citizen.org/pctrade/gattwto/ShrinkSink/shrinksink.htm.

4. See the web site for the Alliance for Sustainable Jobs and the Environment at http://www.asje.org/.

5. David Moberg, "For Unions, Green's Not Easy," *The Nation,* February 21, 2000, p. 18. This article provides valuable background on both positive and negative aspects of labor/environmentalist relations in the United States.

6. The Alliance for Sustainable Jobs and the Environment includes about 400 members of large unions like Teamsters and United Steelworkers and environmental groups Earth First! and the American Lands Alliance. An additional 100 unions and 120 environmental groups have endorsed the alliance. Dave Foster of United Steelworkers, who co-chairs the alliance, said the group was organized because companies "have accumulated so much power that no one government can effectively control them" (Jim Carlton, *Wall Street Journal,* October 4, 1999). The late Earth First! activist Judy Bari helped lay the groundwork for the alliance by her continuing insistence that forest workers should be regarded as potential allies, rather than enemies, of the environmentalists' struggles against corporate destruction of old-growth forests.

7. The course of such coalitions rarely runs smoothly. A major follow-up event was planned at the Kaiser plant in Tacoma, Washington, on March 27, 2000. It was unilaterally cancelled by the Steelworkers without consultation with the allies who were supporting it. For one account of what happened, see Kristian Williams, "Enviro-Labor Unity Takes a Hit as Steel Cancels Tacoma Rally," *Labor Notes* 254 (May 2000): 11.

8. Moberg, "For Unions, Green's Not Easy," p. 18.

9. Moberg, "For Unions, Green's Not Easy," p. 20.

10. Moberg, "For Unions, Green's Not Easy," p. 19.

11. World Commission on Environment and Development, *Our Common Future* (New York: Oxford UP, 1990).

12. See, for example, the keynote speech by Frieder Otto Wolf, then a member of the European Parliament for the Greens, at the Taegu-Round, Taegu, South Korea, October 8, 1999:

> Ecological development, co-development of South and North, and since the Brundtland report "sustainable development" mark decisive dimensions of a deep rethinking that has been achieved in this respect. A similar process is under way with regard to the old, unsustainable, growth-addicted, techno- and male centered model of "full employment" calling for a full employment of a new type, which takes full account of ecological conditions, the demand for a fair exchange between North and South, and feminist demands.

For such a reinterpretation of full employment, see Ken Coates and Stuart Holland, *Full Employment for Europe* (Nottingham: Spokesman, 1995). For a perspective on environmental conversion, see Carl Boggs, "Economic Conversion As a Radical Strategy: Where Social Movements and Labor Meet," in Jeremy Brecher and Tim Costello eds., *Building Bridges: The Emerging Grassroots Coalition of Labor and Community* (New York: Monthly Review Press, 1990), pp. 302–9, and Carl Boggs, *Social Movements and Political Power* (Philadelphia: Temple UP, 1986). See also the many relevant publications of the Worldwatch Institute. Reduction of wasteful military production would surely be an appropriate part of such a conversion process.

13. Energy Innovations, *Energy Innovations: A Prosperous Path to a Clean Environment* (Washington: Alliance to Save Energy et al., 1997).

14. UNCTAD, *Trade and Development Report, 1999* (Geneva, UNCTAD, 1999).

15. The charges are summarized in a letter from the Jubilee 2000 Coalition Afrika Campaign to members of the US Congress dated March 11, 1999, criticizing Rep. Jim Leach's legislation regarding debt relief, which was drawn up with the help of Jubilee 2000 organizations in the North.

Mr. Leach's legislation contains a fatal flaw: it leaves multilateral debt relief in the hands of the International Monetary Fund (IMF), and continues to enforce the current link between access to multilateral debt relief for poor countries and compliance with harsh IMF structural adjustment austerity programs.

For an extended discussion, see Dot Keet, "The International Anti-Debt Campaign—An Activist View from the South—to Activists in the North," AIDC discussion document, available on-line at http://www.aidc.org.za/.

16. Jai Sen, "A World to Win."

17. Walden Bello and Anuradha Mittal, "Dangerous Liaisons: Progressives, the Right, and the Anti-China Trade Campaign," *Focus on Trade* 50 (May 2000).

18. June 1, 2000, speech to National Press Club, broadcast on National Public Radio. Prior consultation with allies might have helped the US trade union movement develop an approach that was less divisive to the movement and ultimately more effective. As journalist Bruce Shapiro put it, "The AFL-CIO and its president, John Sweeney, suffered a failure of nerve about the terms of the debate, retreating from the broad discussion of globalization that exploded after Seattle to narrow rhetoric about protecting American jobs and national security." See Bruce Shapiro, "Early Christmas for Beijing," Salon.com news, May 25, 2000, available on-line at http://www.salon.com/news/feature/2000/05/25/pntr.

19. Summary in Anderson et al., *Field Guide to the Global Economy*, pp. 130–32. Full text available on-line at http://www.web.net/comfront.

20. For one account of this interaction, see Martin Khor, "Seattle Debacle: Revolt of the Developing Nations," in Danaher and Burbach, *Globalize This!* pp. 41–52.

21. Julie Light, "Activists in the Developing World See DC Events as a Watershed in Global Solidarity," Corporate Watch web site, April 17, 2000. Available on-line at http://www.corpwatch.org.

22. In the wake of Seattle, the AFL-CIO Executive Council passed a resolution acknowledging developing country concerns about workers' rights provisions in the WTO and emphasizing that worker rights are "only one element in a broad development agenda" that includes debt relief, development aid, fundamentally changing the agendas of the international financial institutions, and capacity building and technical aid. See "Equitable, Democratic, and Sustainable Development," New Orleans, February 17, 2000 (http://www.aflcio.org/publ/estatements/feb2000/edsd.htm).

23. Jubilee South, Social Watch, and Saprin, "Common Statement of Global Social Movements and Citizens' Organizations on the IFIs and the Management of the Global Economy" (April 2000). The statement was prepared for initial distribution at the Social Summit+5 conference in Geneva in late June 2000. The statement is posted on the Saprin web site at http://www.developmentgap.org/saprin/common_statement.html.

24. For a Southern view of such a "grand bargain," see Jorge G. Casteñeda, *Utopia Unarmed: The Latin American Left After the Cold War* (New York: Knopf, 1993), pp. 443ff.

25. In the wake of the "South Summit" in Havana in April 2000, the G-77 agreed to form a G-77 Political Directorate. Nigerian President Chief Olusegun Obasanjo, chair of the G-77, said, "The G-77 will speak with one voice in a way we have probably not done before." "G77 States Seek to Speak with One Voice," *Financial Times*, April 17, 2000. G-77 representatives were snubbed, however, at the July 2000 meeting of the G-8 in Japan.

26. Third world critics of international labor rights provisions have a responsibility to present alternative means for solving the problem of competition and the race to the bottom within the third world, which has become a crucial barrier to third world development.

27. On the Tobin Tax, see David Felix, "The Tobin Tax Proposal: Background, Issues and Prospects," *UNDP Working Paper* 191 (June 1994); Barry Eichengreen, James Tobin, and Charles Wyplosz, "Two Cases for Sand in the Wheels of International Finance," *Economic Journal* 105 (May 1995): 162–72. Available on-line at http://www.tobintax.org/.

28. In fact,

> The US, with five per cent of the world's population, is currently the biggest single source of global climate change, accounting as it does for a quarter of global greenhouse gas emissions. As the Center for Science and Environment (CSE) points out, the carbon emission level of one US citizen in 1996 was equal to that of 19 Indians, 30 Pakistanis, 17 Maldivians, 49 Sri Lankans, 107 Bangladeshis, 134 Bhutanese, or 269 Nepalis.

> Bello and Mittal, "Dangerous Liaisons," citing Anil Agarwal, Sunita Narain, and Anju Sharm, eds., *Green Politics* (New Delhi: Center for Science and Environment, 2000), p. 16.

Notes to Chapter 5: A World to Win—for What?

1. Michael Elliott et al., "The New Radicals," *Newsweek,* December 13, 1999, p. 36.

2. William Blake, "Milton," *The Poems of William Blake*, W.H. Stevenson ed. (London: Longman, 1971), p. 489. The phrase follows his famous lyric that serves as the text for the song "Jerusalem."

3. The universality of these norms is suggested by the fact that, when challenged, even the heads of the IMF, World Bank, and WTO attempt to justify their institutions in terms of improving the environment, fighting poverty, extending democracy, and the like—the tribute vice so often pays to virtue.

4. For a discussion of communal rights in relation to social movements, see Staughton Lynd, "Communal Rights," in *Living Inside Our Hope*, pp. 89ff.

5. For background and perspectives regarding the full breadth of human rights concerns and their relation to globalization, see the materials of the Center for

Human Rights Education posted on its web site at http://www.pdhre.org.

6. This approach draws on Gramsci's concept of a "historical bloc" that establishes "a synthesis of the aspirations and identities of different groups in a global project which exceeds them all." Perry Anderson, "Problems of Socialist Strategy," in Perry Anderson and Robin Blackburn eds., *Toward Socialism* (Ithaca: Cornell UP, 1965), p. 243.

7. It is often forgotten that, along with the great campaigns of civil disobedience, Gandhi pursued what he called "the constructive program." This was a series of cooperative efforts in what today we would call civil society. Recognizing that British rule limited what such efforts could accomplish, he nonetheless emphasized that people should do what they could to promote literacy, sanitation, equality, and other social goals without waiting for the expulsion of the colonial power. For Gandhi, the constructive program and civil disobedience were complementary. "In any program which envisages the building of a new society, opposition can be expected to arise at various stages and to specific parts of the program, Gandhi argued. It is then necessary to take direct action to remove the obstacle to enable the constructive work to proceed." See Gene Sharp, *Gandhi as a Political Strategist: With Essays on Ethics and Politics* (Boston: Porter Sargent, 1979), Chapter 5, "The Theory of Gandhi's Constructive Program," p. 84.

Drawing on older Polish traditions, the Polish dissident Adam Michnik similarly stressed what was called "constructive work" as an aspect of social change that could be pursued even under repressive conditions. See Adam Michnik, *Letters from Prison and Other Essays* (Berkeley: University of California Press, 1987), pp. 302–3, 316. Modern Islamic movements such as Hamas draw much of their power and support from the wide range of social welfare institutions they have developed to meet needs inadequately fulfilled by established institutions. In the United States, the women's movement has a particularly strong tradition of building such "alternative institutions" as women's health clinics, shelters for battered women, and day-care centers.

Such efforts are intimately related to and can work synergistically with efforts to confront and efforts to reform central institutions. They organize and mobilize people to do what can be done within existing power relations; they provide skills and knowledge that are necessary for people to make their own solutions; and, at the same time, they teach what the effects of existing power relations are and what must be changed to accomplish more.

Notes to Chapter 6: Draft of a Global Program

1. For such a common program for the Americas, see "Alternatives for the Americas: Building a People's Hemispheric Agreement," which is available on-line at http://www.web.net/comfront/alts4americas/eng/eng.html; summary in Anderson et al., *Field Guide to the Global Economy,* pp. 130ff. For a synthesis from the Asian-Pacific network PP21, see Muto Ichiyo, "For an Alliance of Hope," in Brecher et al., *Global Visions,* pp. 147ff. For trade issues, see "WTO—Shrink or Sink!: The

Turn Around Agenda" (http://www.tradewatch.org). For financial issues, see "From Speculation to the Real Economy: An Emerging North-South Labor-Citizens Agenda on Global Finance," the summary of recommendations from the 1998 conference "Toward a Progressive International Economy," sponsored by Friends of the Earth, the International Forum on Globalization, and the Third World Network, in Anderson et al., *Field Guide to the Global Economy,* pp. 128ff. Similar ideas are spelled out more fully in Sarah Anderson and John Cavanagh, *Bearing the Burden: The Impact of Global Financial Crisis on Workers and Alternative Agendas for the IMF and Other Institutions* (Washington: Institute for Policy Studies, April 2000). Many similar proposals are presented in UNDP, *Human Development Report 1999,* and in its previous annual editions. Many significant labor proposals regarding reform of the global economy are available on-line at the AFL-CIO web site: http://www.aflcio.org. Several valuable recent articles on alternatives for the global economy are collected in "Section Four: Ways to Restructure the Global Economy" in Danaher and Burbach, *Globalize This!* See also the wide-ranging synthesis of proposals for reform of the global economy presented by William Greider in a series of articles in *The Nation:* "Global Agenda" (January 31, 2000), "Shopping Till We Drop" (April 10, 2000), and "Time to Rein in Global Finance" (April 24, 2000). For ongoing coverage of third world proposals relating to international negotiations, see the magazine *Third World Resurgence.*

2. H. Res. 479, text available on-line through the US House of Representatives web site: http://thomas.loc.gov/.

For additional information visit Representative Bernie Sanders' (I-VT) web site: http://bernie.house.gov/imf/global.asp. See also "Whose Globalization?" *The Nation,* March 22, 1999, and Ellen Frank, "Bye Bye IMF?: A New Blueprint for the Global Economy," in *Dollars and Sense* 224 (July–August 1999).

3. It is often assumed that these interests are inherently contradictory. For example, it is assumed that rising living standards in the South necessitate lowered living standards in the North or that protection and restoration of the environment imply worse living standards for some or all of the world's people. While neither poverty nor environmental destruction can be reversed without major change worldwide, such change does not require the impoverishment of ordinary citizens of the North. Ending wasteful and destructive use of the world's resources and putting its unused and poorly used resources, particularly its one billion unemployed, to work could largely eliminate poverty and environmental degradation without reducing the real quality of life in the North. Change in consumption patterns will be necessary—for example, reduced dependence on fossil fuels—and the lifestyles of the rich will no doubt need to take a hit, but this does not imply a reduction in overall quality of life for the majority in the North.

4. Starhawk, "How We Really Shut Down the WTO," in Danaher and Burbach, *Globalize This!* pp. 39–40.

5. "WTO—Shrink or Sink!" (http://www.tradewatch.org).

6. See Jeremy Brecher, Tim Costello, and Brendan Smith, *Fight Where You Stand! Why Globalization Matters in Your Community and Workplace and How to Address It*

at the Grassroots (Boston: Campaign on Contingent Work/Commonwork, 2000).

7. Professor Andy Banks of the George Meany Center has proposed that international law mandate that companies recognize and bargain with global union structures composed of unions representing all their workers worldwide. The law would mandate a minimum standard agreement which those structures would have the power to enforce through legally protected local monitoring committees. Personal communication, May 18, 2000. See also Andy Banks, "Monitoring: A Trade Union Perspective" (unpublished paper).

8. There has been considerable debate regarding the appropriate venues for such standards. The international trade union movement, for example, has strongly advocated that such standards be included in the WTO, while third world governments and many NGOs have opposed that proposal and have argued that such issues belong instead in the ILO. In fact, this question is currently moot, since the opposition to incorporating such standards in any international agreement is overwhelming. For the time being, labor rights will have to be imposed on corporations primarily by direct pressure in civil society. As other means for imposing them, such as national policy or international agreement open up, those opportunities should be seized without regard to preconceptions about appropriate venues.

As we argued in Chapter 4, the emerging structures regulating the global economy tend to be multiple and overlapping. And, as Waldon Bello has argued, such pluralism is desirable: "Trade, development, and environmental issues must be formulated and interpreted by a wider body of global organizations [than the WTO], including UNCTAD, the International Labor Organization (ILO), the implementing bodies of multilateral environmental agreements, and regional economic blocs" ("UNCTAD: Time to Lead, Time to Challenge the WTO," in Danaher and Burbach, *Globalize This!* p. 172). Steven Shrybman similarly argues that environmental regulations should be embodied both within trade organizations like the WTO and in international environmental agreements ("Trade Now, Pay Later," in Danaher and Burbach, *Globalize This!* p. 162). Ultimately, such standards should be incorporated in a wide range of rule-making structures. For an extended discussion of issues regarding implementation of labor rights requirements, see Pharis J. Harvey and Terry Collingsworth, "Developing Effective Mechanisms for Implementing Labor Rights in the Global Economy" (Discussion Draft, International Labor Rights Fund, March 9, 1998).

9. "Economic Forum: MAI Foes to Hold Inquiry to View Alternatives," *Vancouver Sun,* September 11, 1998. A discussion paper about this process and its results, "Towards a Citizens' MAI: An Alternative Approach to Developing a Global Investment Treaty Based on Citizens' Rights and Democratic Control" (1998), was prepared by the Polaris Institute in Canada with input from scholars and activists around the world.

10. Proposals include restoring the original Bretton Woods conception that the UN Economic and Social Council (ECOSOC) oversee and coordinate the work of international trade and financial institutions; changing the weighted voting in international financial institutions to correspond to population rather than just investment; adding additional countries to international institution governing boards; establishing elected regional boards of directors; and creating a directly elected Global People's Assembly within the UN system.

11. For the UN Center on Transnational Corporations corporate code of conduct efforts, see Walter A. Chudson, "An Impressionistic Tour of International Investment Codes, 1948–1994," in Orin Kirshner ed., *The Bretton Woods–GATT System* (Armonk, New York: M.E. Sharpe, 1996), p. 177.

12. For detailed suggestions for reclaiming popular control of national governments, see "Democratic Governance," a working paper prepared by Tony Clarke of the Polaris Institute in Canada for the International Forum on Globalization.

13. See Vandana Shiva, "The Greening of the Global Reach," in Brecher et al., *Global Visions,* p. 59.

14. Regional efforts can themselves be transnational. The Great Lakes Regional Compact brings together US states and Canadian provinces for economic development and environmental protection. PP21 has established regional networks of grassroots organizations across national boundaries in several major Asian river valleys.

15. See, for example, Rev. Dr. Robert W. Edgar, "Jubilee 2000: Paying Our Debts," *The Nation,* April 24, 2000, pp. 20–21.

16. For a detailed proposal for such an international investment fund, see Jane D'Arista, "Financial Regulation in a Liberalized Global Environment," paper prepared for the Conference on International Capital Markets and the Future of Economic Policy, Queens' College, University of Cambridge, April 16–17, 1998. For D'Arista's proposals and related work, see the Financial Markets Center web site at http://www.fmcenter.org. As discussed below, the purpose of the Tobin Tax is not simply to raise revenue, but also to put "speed bumps" in the flow of speculative capital. For information on the Tobin Tax and on the campaign promoting it, visit the web site of the Tobin Tax Initiative USA at http://www.tobintax.org. The United Nations Conference on Trade and Development (UNCTAD) predicts that a .25 percent transaction tax would reduce global foreign-exchange transactions by up to 30 percent, while generating around $300 billion in tax revenues. ("Financial Gobalization vs. Free Trade: The Case for the Tobin Tax," *UNCTAD Bulletin,* January–March 1996.) For a discussion of issues around global taxation, also see Howard M. Wachtel, "The Mosaic of Global Taxes," in Pieterse ed., *Global Futures,* pp. 83ff. The Association for the Taxation of Financial Transactions for the Aid of Citizens [ATTAC], an international effort initiated in France, has drawn tens of thousands of people into discussion of the Tobin Tax and related issues. Visit the association's web site on-line at http://www.attac.org.

Peter Dorman has suggested that such funds could provide a transition to a generally more democratic global economy in which securities

> would pass progressively into the ownership of a class of financial intermediaries chartered on condition of extensive public input. Competition between

these institutions and transparency in their operations would preserve incentives for efficient investment, but governments or other agents of the public would increasingly find it in their power to loosely guide or set limits to portfolio choice. This leverage would mitigate pressures toward financial instability and the excessive power of financial markets over democratic institutions … [and] the intermediaries themselves would acquire global scope, providing a venue for democratic processes across national borders.

Peter Dorman, "Actually Existing Globalization," in Preet Aulakh and Michael Schechter eds., *Rethinking Globalization(s): From Corporate Transnationalism to Local Interventions* (New York: St. Martin's Press, 2000).

17. See Steven Shrybman, "Trade Now, Pay Later," in Danaher and Burbach, *Globalize This!*

18. For background on global agricultural issues, see Mark Ritchie, "Rural-Urban Cooperation: Our Populist History and Future," in Brecher and Costello, *Building Bridges*. See also Peter Rosset, "A New Food Movement Comes of Age in Seattle," in Danaher and Burbach, *Globalize This!*

19. See, for example, Oskar Lafontaine, "The Future of German Social Democracy," extract of the text of a speech to the SPD Conference, Hanover, December 2–4, 1997, in *New Left Review* 227 (January–February 1998): 72ff. Lafontaine tried to develop cooperative international policies along these lines during his brief tenure as Germany's finance minister.

20. See the various proposals in Jo Marie Griesgraber and Bernhard G. Gunter eds., *The World's Monetary System: Toward Stability and Sustainability in the Twenty-First Century* (London: Pluto Press, 1996).

21. Proposals for an insolvency mechanism have been developed by Prof. Kunibert Raffer. See Kunibert Raffer, "Applying Chapter 9 Insolvency to International Debts: An Economically Efficient Solution with a Human Face," *World Development* 18: 2 (February 1990): 301ff.

22. Jane D'Arista has proposed one valuable model for such regulation. It involves the regulation of banks and all other financial institutions by national and international regulatory authorities; internationally coordinated minimum reserve requirements on the consolidated global balance sheets of all financial firms; and utilization of reserve requirements to counter cyclical variations in global growth rates. See D'Arista, "Financial Regulation in a Liberalized Global Environment." For D'Arista's proposals and related work, see the Financial Markets Center web site at http://www.fmcenter.org. For more establishment-oriented advocacy of expanded global financial regulation, see John Eatwell and Lance Taylor, "International Capital Markets and the Future of Economic Policy," Center for Economic Policy Analysis, August 1998, and Jeffrey E. Garten, "Needed: A Fed for the World," *New York Times,* September 23, 1998.

Notes to Chapter 7: Self-Organization from Below

1. Keck and Sikkink, *Activists Beyond Borders*. The term *civil society* is sometimes used to characterize such activity, but it is perhaps overbroad, since it is often used to include markets, corporations, and everything else that lies outside the state. The emergence of network forms of organization in social movements parallels the development of what Castells describes as "networked capitalism." See Manuel Castells, *The Information Age: Economy, Society, and Culture*, 3 vols. (Oxford: Blackwell, 1999). Another formulation of transnational social movement organization is Muto Ichiyo's concept of an "alliance of hope." See Muto Ichiyo, "For an Alliance of Hope," in Brecher et al., *Global Visions*, pp. 147–62.

2. "The Non-Governmental Order," *The Economist*, December 11–17, 1999.

3. Keck and Sikkink, *Activists Beyond Borders*, p. 8. Informal networks have probably played a larger role in past movements than those who focus on formal organizations recognize. See Brecher, *Strike!* pp. 275ff.

4. Keck and Sikkink, p. 9.

5. Framing has been defined as "conscious strategic efforts by groups of people to fashion shared understandings of the world and of themselves that legitimate and motivate collective action." See Keck and Sikkink, *Activists Beyond Borders*, p. 3.

6. John Gardner writes:

In a tumultuous, swiftly changing environment, in a world of multiple, colliding systems, the hierarchical position of leaders within their own system is of limited value, because some of the most critically important tasks require lateral leadership—boundary-crossing leadership—involving groups over whom they have no control.

John Gardner, *On Leadership* (New York: Free Press, 1990), p. 98.

7. Starhawk, "How We Really Shut Down the WTO," pp. 36–39.

8. For a similar view, see Naomi Klein, "The Vision Thing," *The Nation*, July 10, 2000, pp. 18–21.

9. For a proposed set of guidelines for such negotiations, see "Respecting Differences While Building Solidarity," *Z Magazine*, January 2000. The guidelines are based on the norms of diversity and solidarity and on the right of people to influence decisions in proportion to how much they are affected.

10. As Frieder Otto Wolf puts it, the NGO movement in its best forms is

building a bridge which makes it possible to give a voice to the local political involvement of grass roots movements everywhere.... The very characteristics of the NGO process as a deliberative movement, taking shape in the development of real communication and discourse, let it make an essential contribution to a productive understanding of the very urgency of the global problems which cannot be solved but in a process of winning active participation and support from the peoples, the women and men of this planet. It therefore helps to discard the delusions of "problem solving dictatorship," in its more traditional authoritarian, as well as in its more refined technocratic forms. The very principles of self-organization and self-determination in the NGO idea should be sufficient to make them aware that these principles cannot survive as a privilege of a more or less self-defined "elite," but only in a process of their being extended to and reclaimed by ever more social and political agents. "Elitism" is, in fact, a recurrent temptation within the NGO movement, but incompatible with its own principles.

Frieder Otto Wolf, lecturer, Freie Universitaet Berlin; former member of the European Parliament for the German Greens. "Beyond the Old Divides, But in a New Predicament," Keynote speech, Taegu-Round, October 8, 1999.

11. "The Non-Governmental Order," *The Economist.*

12. "NGOs should therefore quite consciously strive, ever and again, to put the representative institutions of democracy before their political responsibilities, instead of becoming an accomplice in masking a lack of political responsibility, or even a lack of democracy, on the side of state institutions." Frieder Otto Wolf, "Beyond the Old Divides."

13. "Mobilization for Negotiation Press Conference Calling for Negotiations with the World Bank/IMF," press release, March 13, 2000.

14. May Day once served as such an occasion for the world's labor movement and contributed to the sense of a common global movement. It changed from a symbol of unity to one of disunity in the context of the Cold War, with May Day and Labor Day symbolizing warring factions within the world's labor movement. The spring mobilizations within the United States that began in the Vietnam War era and continued for many years thereafter provided a similar focus. A revival of May Day, with its powerful history both as an environmental and as a labor celebration, seems to be the obvious vehicle. In May 2000, the Pope, with support of Italian trade unions, organized a May Day rally and rock concert dedicated to global solidarity. With such an example before it, perhaps even the US labor movement can overcome its Cold War aversion to May Day.

Notes to Chapter 8: No Movement Is an Island

1. The discussion here is limited to the relation of organized labor movement to the rest of the movement for globalization from below. For discussion of the broader question of how workers' movements can adapt to globalized capital, see Brecher and Costello, *Global Village or Global Pillage,* Chapter 8, and Brecher and Costello, "Labor and the Challenge of the 'Dis-Integrated Corporation.'" A striking new development is the emergence of web sites that provide an independent means of communications for workers in particular corporations worldwide. These are raising significant human rights issues as corporations claim that critical material posted on them violates workers' duty of "company loyalty."

2. See, for example, the resolutions from the February 16–17, 2000, New Orleans meeting of the AFL-CIO Executive Council on "Campaign for Global Fairness" and "Equitable, Democratic, Sustainable Development." Available on-line at

http://www.aflcio.org/publ/estatements/feb2000/edsd.htm. These statements were accompanied by a very important reversal of the AFL-CIO's position to endorse amnesty for undocumented immigrants.

3. Program on International Policy Attitudes, University of Maryland, *Americans on Globalization: A Study of US Public Attitudes—Summary of Findings*, November 16, 1999, principal investigator: Steven Kull. For interpretation of this and related poll data, see *Becoming Global Citizens: How Americans View the World at the Beginning of the 21st Century*, a report prepared by Ethel Klein/EDK Associates for Oxfam America, May 2000.

4. Timothy Egan, "Free Trade Takes On Free Speech," *New York Times*, December 5, 1999, p. 4: 1.

5. Patrick J. Buchanan, *The Great Betrayal: How American Sovereignty and Social Justice Are Being Sacrificed to the Gods of the Global Economy* (Boston: Little, Brown, 1998), p. 61.

6. For examples, see Lizza, "The Man Behind the Anti–Free-Trade Revolt."

7. In the short run, a politician or party that supports global norms against current definitions of national interest is likely to be politically vulnerable, even if the position is in the interest of the country's people in the long run. For that reason, a consistent internationalism is extremely difficult to maintain in a national electoral arena. The movement must remain independent of the electoral arena in part as a way of remaining free from this pressure and free to reflect broader global interests.

8. Gillian Tett, "Japan Seeks Asian Monetary Fund," *Financial Times*, December 16, 1997, p. 10.

9. "Europeans Find Fault With the US," *New York Times*, April 9, 2000 p. 10.

10. Fletcher, "G77 States Seek to Speak with One Voice."

11. In the early 1990s, it was widely believed that the world's dominant tendency was not toward globalization but the formation of a "triad" of rival economic regions built around the US, Japan, and the EU. At the time NAFTA was established, some saw it as a step toward global neoliberalism, but others saw it as a means to strengthen US competitiveness in a struggle with the EU and a Japan-led Asia. George Orwell described such a trilateral conflict in his once-futuristic novel *1984*.

12. Frieder Otto Wolf, "Toward a Comprehensive Critical 'Problematics' of Growth within Economic Policy Theory," contribution to the Conference of European Alternative Economists, Brussels, October 1–3, 1999.

13. Dot Keet, "The International Anti-Debt Campaign."

14. The phrase "globalization from the middle," and many of the ideas in this section, were suggested by Jai Sen.

15. David Croteau has examined the class composition of these movements and the implications of their low level of white working class participation. David Croteau, *Politics and the Class Divide: Working People and the Middle-Class Left* (Philadelphia: Temple UP, 1995).

16. For possibilities of bridging the "class divide" by relating social and economic issues, see Fred Rose, *Coalitions Across the Class Divide: Lessons from the Labor, Peace, and Environmental Movements* (Ithaca: Cornell UP, 2000).

17. For a view emphasizing the role of "the multitude" in future social change, see Chapter 4.3, "The Multitude Against Empire," in Hardt and Negri, *Empire.*

18. See Elizabeth Martínez, "Where Was the Color in Seattle?" *ColorLines* 3: 1 (Spring 2000), and Colin Rajah, "Where Was the Color at A16 in DC?" *ColorLines* 3: 2 (Summer 2000). We address here the specific situation of African Americans. Within those defined as people of color by the US caste system, there is great diversity of historical experience and contemporary situation that needs to be addressed specifically. For Latinos, for example, see Jeremy Brecher, "Popular Movements and Economic Globalization," and the other essays in Frank Bonilla, Edwin Melindez, Rebecca Morales, and Maria de los Angeles Torres eds., *Borderless Borders: U.S. Latinos, Latin Americans, and the Paradox of Interdependence* (Philadelphia: Temple UP, 1998).

19. Hugh B. Price, president and CEO, National Urban League, keynote address to National Urban League Convention, Indianapolis, Indiana, July 24, 1994.

20. Kim Moody, "Mass Strike Around the World: Global Labor Stands Up to Global Capital," *Labor Notes* 256 (July 2000).

21. "Join a Global Fight for Justice." March sponsored by Campaign on Contingent Work, CPPAX, Jobs with Justice, and the National Alliance for Fair Employment, June 29, 2000.

Notes to Chapter 9: Fix It or Nix It

1. For a schematic presentation of some of these weaknesses and contradictions, see the discussion of how movements can fail at the end of Chapter 2.

2. The specificity of the weaknesses of certain kinds of institutions is illustrated by *The Economist*'s observation that

[i]nter-governmental institutions such as the World Bank, the IMF, the UN agencies or the WTO have an enormous weakness in an age of NGOs: they lack political leverage. No parliamentarian is going to face direct pressure from the IMF or the WTO; but every policymaker faces pressure from citizens' groups with special interests. Add to this the poor public image that these technocratic, faceless bureaucracies have developed, and it is hardly surprising that they are popular targets for NGO "swarms."

"The Non-Governmental Order," *The Economist.*

3. Alliance for Democracy, "A Common Agreement on Investment and Society," November 28, 1999. Available on-line at http://www.afd-online.org. Such efforts in civil society have an affinity with Gandhi's notion of a "constructive program."

4. Frederick Douglass, letter to an abolitionist associate, 1849, quoted in *Organize!* (Washington: Seven Locks Press, 1991), p. v.

5. For documents on the MAI campaign, visit the Public Citizen web site at http://www.citizen.org.

6. All-India Congress Committee, *Congress Bulletin* 5 (March 7, 1930). Gandhi was writing to the British Viceroy on the eve of the 1930–1931 civil disobedience campaign.

7. "US Demo Back Indonesian Texaco/Chevron Strikers," *ICEM Update* 41/1999, avilable on-line at http://www.icem.org/update/upd1999/upd99-41.html. Editorial, "Foreign Conservationists Under Siege," *New York Times*, April 1, 2000.

8. For more on the adoption of nonviolent civil disobedience by the American labor movement, see Brecher, *Strike!* pp. 324–25.

9. "The Non-Governmental Order," *The Economist*.

10. "The Non-Governmental Order," *The Economist*.

11. Paul Krugman, "Workers vs. Workers," *New York Times*, May 21, 2000.

12. See Chapter 4 above. Many other forces besides the NGOs led the World Bank to this reversal.

13. For an extended case study of such splits and their impact, along with a vision of an effective "inside/outside" strategy, see Michael Pertschuk's book *Lead Us Not* (forthcoming).

14. See Steven Greenhouse, "Banishing the Dickensian Factor," *New York Times*, July 9, 2000, p. 4: 5.

15. An analysis that focuses on the costs of not conceding can help explain some otherwise puzzling phenomena. When the US Navy decided to name one of its nuclear submarines the *Corpus Christi*, the well-known nonviolent Catholic activist Mitch Snyder protested and announced that he would do anything necessary, unto death, to prevent it. The apparent power of the US Navy was truly infinite relative to that of one pacifist. But the Navy knew that Snyder could use dramatic actions, such as a fast unto death, to focus attention on the threat of nuclear annihilation posed by its submarine program, as well as to embarrass the Navy for its stubborn adherence to its original blasphemy. The Navy finally decided to rename the submarine the *"Corpus Christi,"* indicating by the quotation marks that it referred to the city of that name, rather than to the body of Christ. See "Navy Sub to Be Renamed; Protester Calls Off Fast," *Washington Post*, April 28, 1982, p. C8.

16. "Monsanto Chairman Robert Shapiro Reaffirms Commitment to Biotech; Urges Stakeholders: 'Let's Find Common Ground,'" Monsanto press release, St Louis, Missouri, October 6, 1999. Buried in the release is the statement that

> The exchange with Greenpeace leaders followed an announcement Monday by Monsanto that the company would not commercialize sterile seed technologies. Monsanto made the commitment in response to concerns of experts and stakeholders, including growers in developed countries, about the potential effect of gene protection systems in developing countries.

Change in the balance of forces may also result from changes within the opposition. For example, after decades of resisting regulation, the major US tobacco companies announced that they would accept such regulation and entered negotiations with state attorneys general and a representative of the tobacco control movement. In the course of the negotiations, the tobacco companies accepted many of their critics' proposals and in subsequent legislative negotiations accepted far more. Anti-tobacco activists were stunned by the shift. Why did the shift occur? While only tobacco insiders know for sure, informed observers point to a shift in control of the companies from traditional tobacco men to representatives of Wall Street. The new officials were less interested in selling tobacco than in elevating the price of company stock. This made big changes in the corporations' bottom-line objectives and therefore in their power relations with their opponents. See Pertschuk, *Lead Us Not.*

17. L. Kim Tan, "Human-Rights Group Assails Gap's Saipan Sweatshops," *Boston Herald,* October 29, 1999, p. 33.

18. For a critique of the "fix it or nix it" strategy applied to the IMF and World Bank, see Patrick Bond, "Defunding the Fund, Running on the Bank," *Monthly Review* 52: 3–4 (July/August 2000): 127–40.

19. Maude Barlow and Tony Clarke, *The Battle After Seattle: A Working Paper for Strategic Planning and Action on the WTO: Prepared for Internal Discussion and Feedback by Civil Society Groups in Canada,* January 31, 2000. For the text, visit the Council of Canadians web site at http://www.canadians.org.

20. Chakravarthi Raghavan, "NGOs Launch 'Shrink or Sink' Campaign Against WTO," *The Hindu,* April 10, 2000. The full text is available on-line at http://www.citizen.org/pctrade/gattwto/ShrinkSink/shrinksink.htm.

21. See http://www.citizen.org/pctrade/gattwto/ShrinkSink/shrinksink.htm.

22. "Lori's War: Meet Lori Wallach, Leader of the Anti-WTO Protests in Seattle," *Foreign Policy* 118 (Spring 2000): 40–41.

Index

About the Authors

Jeremy Brecher is the author of ten books on labor and social movements, including the labor history classic *Strike!,* recently published in an updated and revised edition by South End Press. He has coauthored two previous books on globalization: *Global Village or Global Pillage: Economic Reconstruction from the Bottom Up* (South End Press), now in its second edition, and *Global Visions: Beyond the New World Order* (South End Press).

Tim Costello has been a truck driver, workplace activist, and union representative. He is currently director of the Massachusetts Campaign on Contingent Work. He has coauthored several previous books with Brecher, including *Building Bridges* (Monthly Review) and *Global Village or Global Pillage.*

Brendan Smith is a former senior labor, development, and economic policy analyst to US Representative Bernie Sanders (Independent, Vermont), coordinating legislative campaigns in support of international social movements. His articles have appeared in the *Los Angeles Times, Baltimore Sun Times, Advertising Age,* and *Working USA.*

Brecher, Costello, and Smith coproduced the video *Global Village or Global Pillage?* narrated by Edward Asner.

About South End Press

South End Press is a nonprofit, collectively run book publisher with more than 200 titles in print. Since our founding in 1977, we have tried to meet the needs of readers who are exploring, or are already committed to, the politics of radical social change. Our goal is to publish books that encourage critical thinking and constructive action on the key political, cultural, social, economic, and ecological issues shaping life in the United States and in the world. In this way, we hope to give expression to a wide diversity of democratic social movements and to provide an alternative to the products of corporate publishing.

Through the Institute for Social and Cultural Change, South End Press works with other political media projects—Alternative Radio; Speakout, a speakers' bureau; and *Z Magazine*—to expand access to information and critical analysis.

To order books, please send a check or money order to: South End Press, 7 Brookline Street, #1, Cambridge, MA 02139-4146. To order by credit card, call 1-800-533-8478. Please include $3.50 for postage and handling for the first book and 50 cents for each additional book.

Write or e-mail southend@igc.org for a free catalog, or visit our new web site at http://www.southendpress.org.

Related Titles

Global Village or Global Pillage $16
Economic Reconstruction from the Bottom Up (Second edition)
Jeremy Brecher and Tim Costello
ISBN 0-89608-591-0 (paper)

Global Village or Global Pillage? Video $25
Narrated by Edward Asner
ISBN 0-89608-321-1 VHS NTSC

Strike! $22
Revised and Updated Edition (South End Press Classics, Vol. 1)
Jeremy Brecher
ISBN 0-89608-569-4 (paper)

Global Visions $16
Beyond the New World Order
Edited by Jeremy Brecher, John Brown Childs, and Jill Cutler
ISBN 0-89698-460-4 (paper)

Biopiracy $13
The Plunder of Nature and Knowledge
Vanadana Shiva
ISBN 0-89608-555-4 (paper)

Panic Rules! $12
Everything You Need to Know About the Global Economy
Robin Hahnel
ISBN 0-89608-609-7 (paper)

Stolen Harvest $14
The Hijacking of the Global Food Supply
Vandana Shiva
ISBN 0-89608-607-0 (paper)